A Thread in the Tapestry

Sarah Churchill

A Thread in the Tapestry

Illustrated

DODD, MEAD & COMPANY
NEW YORK

PRINTED IN GREAT BRITAIN

To My Mother

Illustrations

7

ACKNOWLEDGEMENTS: The four paintings and the sketch by William Nicholson are reproduced from photographs by A. C. Cooper Colour Limited. Thanks are due to the Imperial War Museum for permission to reproduce the photographs of the groups at Teheran and Yalta, and to Keystone Press Agency Limited for the portrait of Sarah Churchill. The lines from Sarah Churchill's poem 'The Last Farewell' and the complete poem 'Forgive Me' are reprinted from her collection of poems, *The Empty Spaces*, by courtesy of Leslie Frewin.

Preface

In these pages you will not discover hitherto undisclosed secrets about matters that have rocked the world since my father was born in 1874. Others who lived through the varying days have recorded the facts, and made their own evaluations. Neither is this an autobiography. It is a personal and loving testament to the man who was my father.

My mother throughout the years and many changes of home carefully preserved the letters of her children. I never knew that she was doing this. To be handed a bundle of letters late in life is an extremely moving experience. It is like being handed back 'yourself' from the beginning. Your discoveries, your achievements, your failures, your hopes, your survival. As I will say later, in my childhood the details of what 'the grown-ups' discussed passed over my head, but the theme for each generation and each individual in that generation, to face and probe diligently into the problems of the times, was etched indelibly on my heart and mind from the beginning. And, furthermore, to do so 'without fear, favour or affection'.

For verification of my facts I have referred to the following books and people:

My Early Life and *The Second World War* – both by my father:

The War and Colonel Warden by Gerald Pawle, which was based on the recollections of Commander C. R. Thompson, Personal Assistant and Naval Aide to my father throughout the war:

by telephone and letters to my brother Randolph and my sister Mary:

and to

my letters to my mother, to whom this book is lovingly dedicated.

SARAH CHURCHILL

The Last Farewell

SC *We must brace ourselves to the fact*
That we may never meet again.
That the blood and tears that seal this pact
Are not binding
When in later years
This world we know has turned to lead
And among the trebled billions of the dead
We wander through pits of fallen stars
Searching each other
And showing our hearts
As token of our Love
To the sightless eye of space
Let us now become aware
That as in this moment
Of reality's sweet bliss,
All seems unreal and we
Not really here;
So, in that blistering day of Truth,
When among the lonely speechless stars
We wander – bereft of these dear senses that we know –
Unable to communicate –
We may yet . . . be there . . .
WSC *But where?*

A Thread in the Tapestry

THE Queen's town carriage swayed and creaked gently. The horses' hooves were the most decided noise, after them came the distant guns and the drums beating out the relentless precision of the slow march. One could not hear the music.

The silence in the creaking carriage was audible above all. So it had happened: the inevitable Operation Hope Not was nearly over. The days of almost peaceful coma, the Lying in State, and now the last of all journeys that we would ever take with him was on its way.

The curve of Whitehall lay ahead: the Home Office, the Cenotaph, Downing Street, the Treasury, the balcony on the right from which Charles I had made his farewell, the Admiralty, the little Whitehall Theatre of laughter, and Nelson brooding over Trafalgar Square.

The people lining the streets did not seem to be alive, no one batted an eye-lid. I looked at them, and yet our eyes could not meet, for behind their eyes lay their own visions, their own memories.

15

Tribute is a many angled thing. Of necessity much must be sorrow. The sharpness of war, the losses, the doubtful gains and the strange endurance of the human race. I thought of him quite tangibly, lying there in the heavy lead coffin drawn steadily by one hundred and four ratings and four officers of Her Majesty's Navy. I saw again the clear pale colour of his skin, almost luminous in the last days of his life. It was bitterly cold and very grey, so the colours of the flags and uniforms slashed across the scene, carrying the message of love and service far beyond the England that he loved.

England had been to him rather like a mistress that could tease, please, baffle and refuse him. For he thought quite simply that England was the best place on earth and that Christianity in the end was the most enlightened philosophy: and that honour, family and friends were the true accolades of life, and that payment for these was work and duty to your fellow men.

As we passed the Cenotaph, one hundred flags borne by men and women of the wartime resistance movements in France, Denmark and Norway were raised in a last salute to the man whom they considered in their darkest hours a chief and a leader: when, after the funeral they were asked who they were and what they did, they replied: 'We were unknown then, we shall remain unknown now.'

Sarah on her mother's knee,
by John Lavery

ON one of his birthdays a few years before, in answer
to my sister Diana's exclamation of wonderment at
all the things he had done in his life, he said: 'I have
achieved a great deal to achieve nothing in the end.' We were
listening to the radio and reading the always generous news-
paper eulogies. 'How can you say that?' she said. He was
silent. 'There are your books,' I said. 'And your paintings,'
Diana followed. 'Oh yes, yes there are those.' 'And after all,
there is us,' we continued. 'Poor comfort we know at times:
and there are other children who are grateful that they are
alive.' He acknowledged us with a smile and I left the room
to seek out his private secretary, Anthony Montague
Browne, and ask: 'He's just said this, what do you think it
means?'

All our lives we had never tried to copy down the things
that my father had said. Oh, there had been through the
years the few that would try at private luncheons or dinners
to memorize a saying, and who rushed away to scribble it
down because they thought it pungent or memorable, but

we could not: he was our father and you don't follow your father around with a pencil and note book saying 'Do you mind repeating that phrase?' Anyway, I should have thought it almost impossible: for the power when he spoke was such that he riveted your attention and you dared not let your thoughts wander a moment in case you lost the unfolding theme of what he was saying. In the later years when a certain silence descended upon him and he spoke rarely, we would go more frequently to each other, or to Anthony, and ask for an explanation. Anthony understood his directness of thought, and without the probable bias of our emotions.

It was some fourteen years before that Anthony had become my father's secretary: a brilliant young member of the Foreign Service, he had had a fine war record and had been awarded the DFC. In their choice of AMB, the Foreign Office picked not only a man of high intelligence, but also a skilful man. He had ranging knowledge of innumerable subjects, and was ever a patient and amusing lieutenant. We all became very fond of him and during the last years he lightened my father's and mother's load considerably by his always selfless and brilliant service.

We had for a long time, been prepared for my father's death but, strangely, had not realized that with his departure we should also lose so many of those who had served him. I had become attached to all of them and the realization that they were no longer part of us, stabbed me.

I remember once, on returning from America where I had been acting all the hot long summer, my father asked me about my adventures. I told him. He listened intently and when I had finished he asked me simply: 'Do you mind when a show breaks up?'

'Oh yes, terribly,' I said.

'So do I,' he said.

And so did I that grey Sunday morning, prepared yet not prepared for the blinding finality.

Apart from the physical factor of the effort it cost him to speak in the last years – and it was physical – his mind was clear. I think his increasing silence was largely because he felt that he had said all that he could say, written all he could write, done all he could do, and was only waiting with increasing patience and courtesy for the end. It must have been very hard for him.

Sometimes when I used to sit with him in the long afternoons he would repeatedly ask the time. I would tell him. He would sigh deeply. About half an hour later he would ask again. 'What is the time now?' I would tell him. 'Oh Lor',' he would say. My heart would ache for him. I tried to tell him what his living meant to thousands of old and stricken people, that they took heart when they saw him going about his daily life to the House of Commons, and off on his journeys to the sun, where his beloved Muse, Painting, kept him company almost to the end. I said this was perhaps the final test, a Shakespearian concept of life; that a man, unless he is killed in battle or felled by accident or disease, should live his full span, and that however hard it was for him his continuance and patience still brought an inspiration to other men and women who were old, just as he had brought inspiration when they had all been young, and that one day like in Tennyson's *Idylls of the King*, a barge would come and carry him on. . . .

I thought of how he never bore grudges – anyway not for very long. He had an extraordinary sense of loyalty. Once you looked into those strange pallid eyes he could be yours for a lifetime.

I thought of how much fun he had been. Come a grey day he managed somehow to change it. Weather bad. 'Draw the curtains and light the fire; where are my paints?' Miraculously they were to hand. 'Where's that picture I didn't finish?' 'This one?' 'Oh Lor'! Better do something with that.' The fire would crackle and there would be tea and tomato-and-cucumber sandwiches, and Gentlemen's Relish for the gentlemen.

IT was impossible to believe that it was all irrevocably in the past. It was so near, still part of us – even the earliest days of childhood, the things we did then, the people who were with us. People like Nana, Miss Maryott Whyte. It was she whom my mother asked to come and look after us all after my sister Marygold died from a septic throat in August, 1921, at the age of three and a half. My mother could not for many years console herself because she had been away with my father at the time that Marygold became ill.

Nana was my mother's first cousin and had trained as a Norland nurse. It was her task to scold us, get us washed and dressed and as cleaned up as possible. The holidays carefully planned by my mother were a delight. We went to Bucks Mills, Clovelly, and had under Nana's care and kindness the sort of holidays everyone dreams of.

At Chartwell she played many roles: Nana, cousin, confidante and often Father Christmas, when she would don the red robe and white beard and decorate the Christmas tree. One day in full array she leant to put one tiny thing right and was nearly burnt to death ... the smaller children, which included me, were not told and somehow Nana as Father Christmas still appeared.

She was not really *my* Nana, she was Mary's, but she managed to cope with our two very different characters, as well as the eight years difference in our ages.

One day shortly after Mary was born and while my mother was still resting from the event, Diana, Randolph, and I were told that my father was going to drive us out into the country. This was a great day. We clambered into an old Wolseley and with my father at the wheel off we went. He told us on the way down that the purpose of this journey was to inspect a house that he thought of buying in Kent, and he wanted our opinion. We were all thrilled. We must have taken a picnic lunch, but this I don't remember; only the excitement of his showing us Chartwell for the first time.

Chartwell was wildly overgrown and untidy, and contained all the mystery of houses that had not been lived in for many years. We did a complete tour of the house and grounds, my father asking anxiously – it is still clear in my mind – 'Do you like it?' Did we like it? We were delirious. 'Oh, do buy it! Do buy it!' we exclaimed. 'Well, I'm not sure. . . .' He kept us in anxious suspense.

We were all so excited when we set off for home that my father couldn't make the car start. Help was solicited and an amazing number of people helped to push the Wolseley about a quarter of a mile along a slight incline so that we could have the benefit of the subsequent decline to start the reluctant engine. I noticed the people helping were very red in the face, but ours were redder still when it was discovered that the ignition was off and the brake on.

These two important things adjusted, we never looked back and sped merrily homeward, all of us badgering my father to buy the house. Not until we reached Parliament Square did he divulge that he had already bought it.

Our excitement was great, and his must have been too, because he took a wrong turning round the square and was promptly stopped by a policeman. We all looked very contrite about the whole thing and were allowed to go home – the right way this time – to my mother, who was waiting to hear if the children approved of Chartwell.

Chartwell was originally a small, Henry VIII manor house built out of red brick and in its original state must have been a charming and pleasing house. Subsequent owners had added on wings, not too successfully.

For practical reasons my mother had to make her own additions and Chartwell today is a tall, rather ungainly house, but its attraction lies in its superb setting and because, since it is built on the side of a sharply sloping hill, the rooms have different and dramatic levels. So if the house is not strictly beautiful outside, it is a dream inside – due to my mother who had pushed and prodded the reluctant walls about, as well as a very reluctant architect.

Bold and imaginative as my father was in everything he undertook, he had fallen in love with Chartwell at first sight and thought it needed no improvement. He watched with apprehension my mother's determined actions. Away went the mysterious but suffocating rhododendrons, ivy and goodness knows what other creepers that had tried to eat and smother the house in its twenty years of emptiness.

Trees too had to fall to give air and light and view. Down and away went the green intruders. On the removal of a really remarkable cedar tree to make room for the east wing I remember my father muttering a studied, very audible aside: 'If you go on like this, Clemmie, we had better rename the house One Tree Hill.' Undeterred, my mother continued subtly getting me at least on her side by saying to no one in particular: 'Creepers tend to undermine the mortar of the house. Besides there will be earwigs in the children's bedrooms.'

If my father was at first alarmed at my mother's activities of tree and shrub clearing, he soon caught this fever for improvement and construction himself. During the 'thirties, when he was in the political wilderness, he found time, despite his enormous literary output, to build a wall round the kitchen garden, doing the major part of this work entirely by himself. He also built two cottages and organized an elaborate system of waterworks to feed the golden carp pools and miniature waterfalls in the water garden. As if this wasn't enough he built a swimming pool complete with heating arrangements, the boiler room of which was said to be sufficient to heat the Ritz.

'I lived mainly at Chartwell, where I had much to amuse me. I built with my own hands a large part of two cottages and extensive kitchen-garden walls, and made all kinds of rockeries and waterworks and a large swimming-pool which was filtered to limpidity and could be heated to supplement our fickle sunshine. Thus I never had a dull or idle moment from morning till midnight, and with my happy family around me dwelt at peace within my habitation.'[1]

All these endeavours were not achieved without considerable and sometimes costly mistakes. My father was not

[1] THE GATHERING STORM by Winston S. Churchill (Cassell).

only the instigator of all these schemes but the sole architect, and always one of the labourers.

We were fortunate enough to have a natural spring in the valley but it was quite a humble thing and if it had been left to its own devices it would have trickled unnoticed through the bottom of the valley with perhaps a few soggy patches to announce its presence. The former occupant had dammed it at one point, and there was already a large and pleasant lake. 'Why only one?' asked my father.

Immediately another lake above the dam was excavated. But he then decided both these lakes, with their muddy bottoms and weeds, were too dangerous for us to swim in, so it was abandoned to the swans and wild fowl, and another dam was built even higher up the valley. This lake was cemented to make it clear and safe for swimming but something went wrong again. The pool tended to leak or seep, even at one point threatening to slide down the hill. So once again this too was abandoned, and another pool was built on the other side of the valley nearer to the house. As the flow of the spring was too small, company water had to be added and an electric pump installed to send the water, rather like a stage army, round and round from the large lake up to the water garden, through a filter to the swimming pool, and back.

We, the children, thought it was all very exciting. Perhaps it was just as well that my mother was away on a long cruise to the West Indies at the time.

The beautiful valley went through considerable scarring and at one point, owing to a mistake in somebody's arithmetic, there arrived an excessive quantity of cement, a cement-mixer, and a magical product called bitumen, apparently the cure-all for leaking pools. My father, never averse to a pun, taking in the scene of chaos and desolation with apparent calm, remarked to the gentlemen who dumped the stuff on us: 'Oh, is this the bit-you-mean?' They stared at him and left.

However, the 'architect' triumphed in the end, and by the following summer the scars on the turf had disappeared, and we frolicked in the heated pool or sat in the shade listening to the tinkle of water flowing gently over the falls, and were reminded by my mother to turn off the electric pump whenever we or the guests left the garden.

The wall round the kitchen garden seems to have presented fewer problems, perhaps because the foundations were laid professionally, and the wall built to about knee height first. From then onward my father took charge of all bricklaying. He had, of course, a professional mate, but I was his second mate. It was my duty not only to hand him bricks and see there was a constant supply of moist cement but to see that the plumbline was 'plumbing' the way it should. We had a spot of trouble, naturally, in the beginning.

One day when a particular section of the wall was decidedly wiggly and my father and I were contemplating this in deep silence, a guest passing by said: 'Oh, Winston, that bit is very crooked.'

'Any fool can see what's wrong,' barked my father. 'But can you see what's right?' The guest sped quickly to another part of the garden while my father and I returned loftily to our labours.

Pets were very important and we had quite an assortment. There were my father's polo ponies on which we learned to ride; there were cows and sheep and chickens, but it was not a working farm, because my father had very strong views about no animal being slaughtered for food once he had said 'Good morning' to it.

I remember an old ram of which he became very fond. He had known it as a lamb and fed it from the bottle. When it grew up it was an absolutely horrible beast and for some extraordinary reason it was called Charmayne. I believe it had been doctored in the hope that it would be less fierce, but things didn't work out that way at all. It used to butt everybody and we children were nervous of the beast. My mother tried to persuade my father to get rid of it, but my father wouldn't. He said: 'How ridiculous, you don't have to be frightened; it is very nice and knows me.'

However, one unfortunate day Charmayne, apparently not realizing the faith my father had placed in him, butted him sharply in the back of the knees, and knocked him flat. Charmayne was never mentioned again and was banished from Paradise!

Banishment was the main form of punishment in our childhood, sometimes our pocket money would be stopped. But we all stood in Victorian awe and respect of both parents. We were just ordinarily naughty children and it was thought that Reason should explain to us the nature of our fault.

It was certainly for me sufficient ordeal to visit either my father or my mother to be reprimanded, and it was a very serious matter to be banished to your room. No physical force was ever used, except by one or two nurses when we were very small. I remember one nurse racking a teaspoon in Randolph's mouth until two of his tiny teeth fell out because he had sucked at his spoon too long, but it was many years before my parents knew of this.

Mary had a pug. At one point Pug became desperately ill. Mary was in tears, I was in tears. My father was greatly upset at our distress, and although he really thought that poetry, though enjoyable, was a minor sort of thing – prose being very much more important – he composed this ditty for Mary and me, which went this way and which we all chanted while Puggy was ill:

> *Oh, what is the matter with poor Puggy-wug?*
> *Pet him and kiss him and give him a hug.*
> *Run and fetch him a suitable drug,*
> *Wrap him up tenderly all in a rug,*
> *That is the way to cure Puggy-wug.*

Long and golden were the summer evenings. On the valley side of the house there is a carefully mown lawn some hundred and fifty yards long by fifty yards wide. It is edged by a small grey stone parapet two feet high on which we often sat to sun ourselves.

This at any age was quite dangerous, as the drop the other side was anything from twelve to twenty feet. Below lie the valley and lakes, and the whole scene except to the south and south-west is surrounded by a belt of magnificent beeches. On this open side lies the dramatic view of the Weald of Kent. Summer and winter this view, framed by the beeches, green or a blaze of copper, is to my mind – and I know it was to my father's – one of the most beautiful views in England.

The drop between the lawn and the meadow was to become very important to me, for the simple reason that I whirled myself over it during a game of blind man's buff with my Romilly cousins. I must have been about eleven years old. Luckily I took this Nijinsky leap at the lowest point of the drop, but an unexpected crash of twelve feet, blindfolded, is a very horrible experience. It could also have have been a serious one – fortunately it was only painful.

I did not break anything, but tore the front muscles of my shoulders in an instinctive effort to right myself. I had to be in bed for some time, but since it was the holidays, I was comforted by my cousin Peregrine Churchill with whom I had been passionately and devotedly in love, since the age of four.

My first recollection of Pebbin was lying in adjoining cots, so close that we could hold fingers through the bars. We were two, only a few months separated us. There is a considerable difference of ages in our family. Not now, of course, but as children a difference of three, five, and eight years separates you very much. So it was natural that Pebbin and I should be thrown much together, even more so after the death of my sister Marygold when I was about six.

We are not a family who ring each other up every day, and we are notoriously bad letter-writers to each other – except under extreme crisis like the need for a temporary loan or a national emergency. We do not ask questions of each other or pry into each other's affairs. Tentative and delicate feelers may be extended; if not taken up they are immediately withdrawn, for we believe passionately in the privacy of our lives and other people's.

My father had built for Pebbin and me a house in a tall elm. It was a two-storeyed affair; it was a good twenty feet high, and was reached by first shinning up a rope and then climbing on carefully placed struts between the four stems of the elm.

Our privacy was strongly protected as my father placed a special cross-bar half-way up the tree, and this stopped anyone bigger than ourselves climbing any further.

Our playground was the water garden. With the water-falls, bamboo clumps, flowering bushes, it was a fantastic playground for any child. The games we played had a continuity through the years. Principally, Pebbin was a famous detective, and I his rather stupid secretary Miss Smith. We acted all the characters with vigour. Strange, weird cries of fear and strangulation were often heard, but if the other children tried to spy on us, with animal instinct we would know and freeze. When we were exhausted by these boisterous games we would climb to our house in the tree for seclusion and rest.

While Pebbin and I were scampering about in the water garden or the lofty seclusion of our tree-top, the other children led by Johnny Churchill got up to the most extra-ordinary antics. Johnny was a very fine athlete. He would do the most daring things, running along the edge of the roof, bounding out of windows: this was very difficult for Randolph who did not possess this athletic prowess, but he wouldn't give up and sometimes he had some nasty falls in trying to follow Johnny, and often my heart would be in my mouth.

Always during the holidays we had lunch with my parents no matter who were the guests, first at a small round table, then when we were old enough at the larger one.

My mother and father have always liked round tables.

Unquestionably they are the best for conversation and ideal for family life, as everyone can see everyone and no one gets left out.

Conversation was meant to be general; that did not mean everyone was to speak at once, though of course it frequently resulted in that. We were taught not to mumble – 'Say what you have to say, say it clearly or don't say it at all,' were the directions. I found this alarming, and it will test the belief of my friends in later life to learn that I was a silent child. So silent that I became a focal point of teasing – 'Sarah hasn't said a thing – come on, Sarah, say something.' There would be a moment of misery and confusion but this was never allowed to go on long. 'Sarah is an oyster, she will not tell us her secrets,' my father would say, and the trend of conversation would pick up again and I would be allowed to sink into my dreams once more.

Randolph showed from early on the sprightly and original way we know today of turning a conversation to his advantage. This delighted my father and as Randolph grew older, glorious rows would shake the room. I was never to have verbal facility with my father, though this was somehow not to prevent an understanding between us on nearly every subject and situation all our lives.

As I have said, it was important to state clearly and briefly what it was you wished to discuss. Muddle-headedness irritated him, also a stumbling delivery. As I matured I literally would 'tidy my mind' before talking to him seriously. He never failed to appreciate my effort. 'Thank you, my darling, thank you. You have put it very clearly.'

On most occasions, however, if I really wanted to say or ask anything important, I could not trust my tongue to get it right and I would scribble him or my mother a note. This note-writing became in the end, certainly among the women, quite a family procedure on matters of importance, for as life progressed and my father became once again increasingly involved in the great events that were so soon to involve us all, it became the best way of communicating, and the least tiring and time-absorbing for him.

As I grew older I naturally took more interest in the conversations, which ranged through every subject imaginable. I remained silent, but was increasingly fascinated, and subconsciously I must have absorbed a great deal.

The guests were varied and many; people of greatly differing views came to visit my father. As time went on, it became apparent that he considered all was far from well. A shadow was growing over the former sunlit scene. The serious and emphatic tones of my father's voice would ring out across the lawn: 'In twenty short minutes the enemy, on leaving the coast of France, can be overhead, menacing, in a way never before contemplated, the security of our island!' And a fear would grip my heart.

We never doubted who the enemy was, but Britain had been lulled into complacency, only to awake at the crisis of Munich, when she became sharply and bitterly divided.

Despite the fact that my father had been out of office, and I had heard people referring to him as though he were finished, it was at this time I realized he was no ordinary man. I had been, from an early age, conscious of the importance of some of the guests that came to the house to seek, to argue, to disagree. But from fourteen onwards I was completely aware of the even greater importance of the

The Moon Goddess,
a portrait of her mother by Sarah Churchill

man who was my father. I had stepped back, so to speak, and began to develop a power to see and hear him with a certain detachment.

My love for him grew and my hero-worship of him never lessened, but now it was tangible. I wanted to be in the league of people who, if they could not help, at least understood where he was trying to go with an idea. I tried to train myself to think; not the things he thought, but the way he thought, and would apply it to certain problems as a practice, so that even if one didn't speak one was in silent step with him, and he could go on thinking with the knowledge that those listening to him were keeping up with his thoughts.

He flourished in this atmosphere, and when with a trusted audience he would let them see his mind leaping and ranging around a problem in a breathlessly spectacular way. And not always, of course, from his own or even his final viewpoints.

It used to amuse me to see the look of bewilderment and shock on the face of some guest not used to this display as my father would elaborate on the possible end to some idea or course of action, playing it with such conviction that the guest would assume it was to be his policy.

'Oh, but you can't possibly think or do such a thing,' they would expostulate.

'I can *think* anything,' my father would reply. 'What I *do* is, of course, a different matter,' and he might maddeningly never tell us what it was he proposed to do, but shoot off on some other tangent of possibility.

IN that silent coach I thought about the friends he had
known through his long life . . . a few of them still with
us, most of them gone.

One of my favourites was Lawrence of Arabia. I knew
him as T. E. Shaw. He would arrive on his motor-bicycle
from a nearby Air Force station on Sunday afternoons for
tea. He never announced his arrival. Many Sundays I would
be disappointed by his absence, but suddenly, like all good
things in childhood, he would surprise us and be there.

He was delightful with children and extremely fond of
my mother. He was a small, slight man; his fine head looked
almost out of proportion. He had a very soft voice and the
noisy extrovert Churchills were silenced by his quiet personality, and we would all listen in pin-drop silence to what
he had to say. I remembered my father sitting back watching
him with a half smile and letting him run the conversation.
He had a great admiration for him, though once he shrewdly
remarked that 'Lawrence, despite all his profound dislike

of publicity, had a remarkable way of backing into the limelight.' But withal my father counted him among the most remarkable men of the twentieth century and paid this tribute to him when he died: 'We shall never see his like again. His name will live in history. It will live in the annals of war . . . It will live in the legends of Araby.'

Then there was the great day when Charlie Chaplin arrived. We children adored his films, and were in a fever of excitement. But we were astounded when we saw him. He didn't look like the Charlie Chaplin we knew. Instead there appeared a rather good-looking, desperately serious man with almost white hair.

During lunch my father tried to draw him out about his work, but this did not suit Chaplin at all for he wanted to discuss politics. This did not suit us at all as we wanted to know about his work and the art of comedy.

However, in deference to our guest my mother had turned the conversation on to a political discussion, which I regret to say my father found extremely boring. After some time my father, determined to get Mr Chaplin back on the subject of acting, asked him in a suitable pause what role he planned to play next. 'Jesus Christ,' replied Mr Chaplin.

After a moment's pause my father asked: 'Have you cleared the rights?'

After another pause my mother skilfully steered the conversation back to politics again.

We hid our disappointment as best we could but he must have sensed it, for just as he was about to leave he said: 'Is there a walking stick?' – 'Yes,' we said and pointed to the hall cupboard. He disappeared into it and emerged with a bowler hat and a stick. In a twinkling of an eye there was the little figure that had endeared itself to us and to millions all over the world.

And this wasn't the only thing he did, he gave some very amusing mimicry of other actors. One, never to be forgotten, of John Barrymore rehearsing 'To be or not to be' from *Hamlet* while picking his nose. The day was made for us and we were sorry to see him go.

I suppose one of the most brilliant talkers and fascinators of the world was the first Lord Birkenhead. He was my brother's godfather and when any special guest connected with one of the children, like a godfather, came to the house, all the other children played up tremendously so that that particular child was the centre of attention. Randolph was always strangely nervous on these occasions, as he had a very great admiration for Lord Birkenhead. Randolph would give us strict instructions as to what we should do, and what we were to say and not to say: anyway we all listened to the sharpening up lecture and of course would play up, as indeed he would do if any of the other children were meant to be the centre of attention.

My godfather was Eddy Marsh, one of the most delightful people I have ever met. I was never, unfortunately, to know him too well. Shyness again, perhaps. When I grew up he made many efforts to know me, but my inability for facile conversation made us both really very uncomfortable, although I appreciated his wide artistic knowledge and the beautiful translations that he did of the *Fables of La Fontaine*.

Then there was of course the dear 'Prof', Professor Lindemann, later Lord Cherwell, who was my father's scientific adviser for many years. He was a vegetarian, a bachelor and a teetotaller, all of which things my father greatly deplored, but which slight imperfections he tolerated because of the value he placed on the Prof's splendid mind and friendship. He was part of our Chartwell life. It is hard to remember an occasion on which he was not present. His exterior was conventionally forbidding: the domed cranium, the close-cropped iron-grey hair which had receded as if the brain had pushed it away, the iron-grey moustache, the sallow complexion, the little sniff which took the place of what normally would have been a laugh; yet still he could exude a warmth that made scientific thinking unfrightening. He was deeply loved by all who studied under him at Oxford, and though his appearance belied it, his parties could be fun. They remained to his undergraduates some of the most brilliant and enjoyable evenings of their lives.

It was principally to the Prof that my father owed his remarkable insight into the heart of abstruse scientific matters. My father never pretended to professional expertise and, while expanding on every possible theme with a trusted audience, he always passed the ball when there was a mind that he respected or relied on for information, listening with the same force as he gave to speech and action. From a session with the Prof he would manage to grasp the kernel of the matter being discussed and from there onwards with his own brilliance he could work out almost exactly how things were likely to turn out.

Prof had the gift of conveying a most complicated subject in simple form. One day at lunch when coffee and brandy were being served my father decided to have a slight 'go' at Prof who had just completed a treatise on the Quantum Theory. 'Prof,' he said, 'tell us in words of one syllable and in no longer than five minutes, what is the Quantum Theory?' My father then placed his large gold watch known as 'the turnip' on the table. When you consider that Professor Lindemann must have spent many years working on this major theme, it was quite a tall order. However, without hesitation, like quicksilver, he planted the principle and held us spellbound. When he had finished we all spontaneously burst into applause.

Many people forgot that the Prof had been a man of action. In the first war he used to turn up at Farnborough wearing a dark suit and stiff collar and put his theories to the test in early and somewhat perilous flying machines. He is said to have been one of the first pilots to recover from a spin which for many years was thought to be a final and fatal manœuvre.

Brendan Bracken was another part of our life at Chartwell. Sunday became known as 'Brendan Day'. He was in complete contrast to the Prof. A redheaded Irishman, of booming character and voice, he would instil and embrace all with his warm-hearted energy. He talked like a fountain, without pause, a considerable achievement in our household. Sometimes one discounted a great deal of what he said. Later, however, if you reflected on it, you realized how remarkably well informed and far-sighted he was. He was of course a brilliant Minister of Information during the war. He allied a stringent practical common sense with a shining loyalty to his friends. All sorts of stories circulated about Brendan's origins. One of them was even that he was an illegitimate son of my father's! Brendan took a certain pleasure in this and similar stories and did not bother to deny them, but rather deliberately chose to remain an enigma. Both the Prof and Brendan would shower us children with delightful gifts, seeming magically to know what each of us wanted at that particular time.

I suppose the most compelling and consistently fascinating character in our life was my father's old friend Lord Beaverbrook. The course of their 'true love' certainly did not run smooth, and there were periods when they were barely on speaking terms. Yet throughout there ran a thread of intense personal regard. Max was a strange and difficult man to know. He inspired either deep affection or hatred. You certainly couldn't be indifferent to him.

Thinking back on the many gay occasions when he was a guest of my father's, whether at Chartwell or in London, or on holiday picnics at Marrakech, I know of no one, apart from my father, who could be such a brilliant story-teller, or who could command such complete attention from his audience. His vibrant being was never more brilliantly expressed than during the desperate days of the war, and the story of his formidable success in providing, it seemed miraculously, the sorely needed aircraft, is well known. My father saw and deeply respected his disregard for personal suffering. Max Beaverbrook had to rise above repeated and devastating attacks of asthma throughout his life. No one will ever forget his gallant last speech on his eighty-fifth birthday within a few days of his death; and the sombre and deliberate way in which he concluded. He had been praised for many things, but perhaps the compliment dearest to his heart was that he was Master of his Trade – in other words a great newspaperman. I feel that his reply was indicative of the flashes of the 'Moment of Truth' which all great men must have: 'It is time for me to become an apprentice once more. I am not certain in which direction, but somewhere, some time, soon. . . .'

Another friend flashed to my mind: the Duke of Windsor, whom my father had stoutly tried to defend and advise throughout the crisis of the abdication. My father was a monarchist. The right of kings has long been tempered to constitutional monarchy and he believed in the sanity and the necessity of this separating of crown from power, but he also believed that constitutional monarchy still entitled the monarch to undying allegiance and service from his people. When destiny demanded a crisis on the personal rights of Edward VIII he was there to defend, explore and advise. All his life he considered he should offer what service he could, in bad times as well as in good, to the people he served.

I assume this would have been his role in whatever age he might have lived, but even more powerful perhaps than this traditional feeling was his shining sense of friendship. Many times in life was he to put himself into question and jeopardy for his friends. As he gave, so he received in turn, life-long friendship and devotion from his friends.

During the 1930s – the years in the political wilderness – in spite of all his outdoor activities, my father completed *The World Crisis*, wrote *Marlborough* and laid the plans for *A History of the English-Speaking People*. Every time he finished a volume he would spend an enjoyable evening signing copies to send to his closest friends. They would of course send their thanks promptly to the exuberant author. As the years went on and the number of volumes steadily increased it probably became a little difficult for everyone to vary his thanks. On the completion of the volumes of *Marl-*

borough, my father received a note from a friend of royal lineage which said: 'Dear Winston, Thank you for your book, I have put it on the shelf with the others.' The family, on being told this by my mother, collapsed in laughter. It evoked for us the famous story of what the then Duke of Gloucester is supposed to have said to Mr Gibbon: 'Another damned thick square book! Always scribble, scribble, eh Mr Gibbon?'

Naturally not all of the guests were of political importance, some were just my father's and mother's personal friends, and Sunday luncheon was nearly always a most amusing affair. Occasionally, of course, one got someone who didn't fit in. There was one lady who was an attractive but celebrity-eating hostess, well known for her persistence in her social endeavours. About the time she was invited, Mary was beginning to take a great interest in everything. She was now sitting at the big table and one day she overheard my mother saying to my father that this lady was coming to lunch, whereupon there was an exclamation of horror from my father who mumbled something to the effect, 'Oh Lor', that lion-huntress.' Well, lunch and the lady arrived. It was a delicious affair as usual, with lots of cold beef or lamb and salad. Afterwards over coffee and brandy there fell a moment's silence of contentment. Mary seized the opportunity to make some attempt at conversation, as we had been taught to do, and turning graciously to this particular guest piped up loudly and clearly: 'Oh do tell me, have you caught any lions recently?' We were all bundled out into the garden and later told it was perhaps after all better to wait until we were spoken to.

During this time Pebbin and I were growing up very fast and a certain formality descended upon our relationship. One day I noticed he was bringing up planks of wood into the house in the tree. I suppose we were about fifteen. I wondered if there was to be some new extension, but on the contrary, it was to make a partition between the main room and the bay window. When I asked, 'Why?' he said: 'This is my study, there are times when men have to be alone.'

About a year later he was to have an acute appendicitis. I was not happy about his appendix, but I was happy for the occasion to rush up to Cromwell Road, where he lived, to be at his bedside. I took with me what I could of our past existence: the notes that the detective had handed to Miss Smith and which she had so badly typed, a rusty nail which of course solved that very important occasion in the water garden, when I believed a certain villainous Mr Woo was about to attack me from the bamboo, and a piece of string which had inevitably saved our lives at some point or other. I laid them on his bed and I remember very clearly to this day that he said: 'Sarah, we can no longer play games, we are grown up.' This was the first time in my life that I had been rejected. And I have never liked Cromwell Road since.

Many years later, when of course this childhood hurt had healed, I told my father this story. When I had finished, I looked up at him and to my surprise found his eyes bright with tears.

I LOOKED up now at my mother and wondered what thoughts were flashing through her mind.

The carriage was approaching the Strand. My thoughts strayed to the Adelphi Theatre where I had made my first appearance on the stage. At the time I did not know that directly opposite, where there is now a department store, was the site of the old Tivoli Theatre at the turn of the century, where as a young man my father had gone and enjoyed to the full the robust music-hall songs and comedy of the day. I thought of our favourite songs, learnt in childhood, and how when we were alone we would coax him to sing us his particular favourites. The names of Marie Lloyd, Little Tich, Vesta Tilley, Chirgwin, the One-Eyed Kaffir, George Robey come easily to mind, and there was one which always caused great hilarity in our house, though I was never able to trace who sang it. It went something like this:

> *I wanted to get married*
> *Like a lot of foolish men.*
> *Found a girl, got engaged,*

Got married there and then.
But after it was over
I got taken down a peg,
Her hair, her eyes, her teeth
Were false
And she'd a wooden leg.
But I can't change it,
I can't change it,
It was a great surprise to me
Half a woman and half a tree
But I'll chop her up for firewood
In the sweet by and by.

There were lots of other verses but another one that stuck in my memory was:

When I got home the other night
The nurse was at the door.
She said 'You've got another one,
That makes it just a score.
It is a pretty little girl
T'will fill your heart with joy.'
I cursed it to the devil
For what I wanted was a boy.
But I can't change it,
I can't change it,
I asked the doctor, he said 'No',
I asked the nurse, she said:
'I can't, I won't.
I don't intend to try,
But I hopes you have another
In the sweet by and by.'

My father's memory was, of course, one of the most incredible things, and we as children were taught to memorize as much as we could. Great lashings of poetry were stashed away inside us and on the long summer evenings, when we would be sleeping out in the garden, it became fun to see how long we could keep reciting poetry and even bits of famous prose. Randolph excelled at this and together as a family we had a good record, and to this day we all still remember many things that we have not thought of for many years. My father decided it was a good practice. He would say that you never know what circumstances – unfortunate circumstances – you may find yourselves in, in life. There may be no books. You may have to wait patiently in boring or worse still, uncomfortable, situations. Close your eyes and call to mind the words of poets who have left you a legacy. Perhaps when he spent those few days down the mine, as an escaped prisoner of war in South Africa, where he had to stay in total darkness, saving the candles his rescuer had given him, he consoled and strengthened himself this way, thus mastering what must have been an interminable time.

In the early thirties it was fashionable to send girls like myself to Munich after they had finished their ordinary education.

My mother, who speaks French and German fluently, wanted me to have another language at my fingertips, but sixteen and seventeen years of age are impressionable years. My father viewed with grave concern the rise of Hitler and his Brownshirts and feared I might be swept up in the enthusiasm of Fascism, which is what happened to my cousin, Unity Mitford.

And so I was sent to a school in Paris run by three Protestant sisters – the Mesdemoiselles Ozanne. I was extremely happy there. I spoke French better than average as my mother had made an effort to see that I – and indeed all her children – did. A succession of French governesses had haunted our holidays since I could remember, and had dinned into our heads the pleasures of learning another language without tears – except occasionally from the governess!

My stay in Paris was to be the most enjoyable part of my education. We had excellent professors from the Sorbonne: Monsieur Bidault, who taught history, was later to become French Foreign Minister, and Monsieur Clarac, who taught literature, became the head of the Sorbonne. After the rigours of an English boarding school this interlude seemed very civilized, and I learned quite a bit. All subjects were taught in French, not a word of English was spoken. After four terms I was considered 'finished' and came back to Chartwell to prepare for my debut.

Four terms in Paris, however, had not altered my shyness; to a degree it had enhanced it. It was in Paris that I started to write. My childhood fantasy was over, but nothing had filled the gap. The world I was leaving had been golden and secure, the one I was going to sounded ominous. Loneliness is normal in adolescence; but nevertheless – as all who have passed through it know – it can be stabbingly real. I still enjoyed my life at Chartwell, but the emptiness between childhood and womanhood had not been filled. I sighed, and loitered about the house.

I acquired my sister Diana's gramophone. Diana was now married. At first I played her sentimental selection over and over again. I then acquired some records of my own. But however quietly you play a gramophone, somehow the plaintive wails leak through a house.

My father always had an abhorrence of whistling. We were never – no one was ever – allowed to whistle. He was extremely sensitive to noise. Working at tremendous tension in his room, either a monotonous noise like a dripping tap, or a distant hammering, or a babble of voices could make him very angry. Understandably, when you consider the breadth of the structure of the work he was undertaking, even a stealthy footstep or whisper would annoy him. 'Who's there?' – 'Come in.' – 'Speak up.' – 'What do you want?'

The great concentrative powers which were his must have been so alive that he was not like some artists who can lose themselves completely. It must have been as if the whole of his mind was aware, and nearby sounds could distort themselves and intrude on his consciousness. He remained in tune with the daily world while pursuing some theme or probing and marshalling facts of some battle or argument of long ago.

Through these moments the wail of my hand-wound gramophone must have penetrated like a file on a too smooth surface. There would be a bellowing roar. The household, released from trying to tip-toe, would now stampede to knock at my door.

'Miss Sarah, your father is objecting to the noise.' Conscience-stricken I would 'kill' my gramophone. At lunch he would beam around at everyone.

'What did you do this morning?' he would ask me. 'Did you go out?'

'No.'

'It's a nice day.'

'Yes.'

'What did you do?'

'I played my gramophone.' He would look at me ponderously for a moment, then smile and say, 'Hummph, Sarah's Solace.'

This was the time (1933) that my parents had their twenty-fifth wedding anniversary. Their friends commissioned William Nicholson to paint a picture of them together. William Nicholson I consider my fairy godfather.

He arrived with his box of paints and stayed many months to paint – not only my mother and father, but our cat and the black swans, and he left innumerable funny little drawings about the house. A family favourite is still one of a lady in Grecian dress, leaning pensively on a pillar with a chubby boy at her feet. The caption: 'Necessity, endeavouring to recollect who was the father of Invention.' My mother bought nearly all that William Nicholson drew during the time he was with us. 'Out of my own pin money,' she said proudly. William Nicholson was a painter of infinite sensitivity and one of those souls 'the Gods' give to a distracted world.

He found me one day mooching to 'Sarah's Solace' in the dining-room. I was dancing and dreaming and conjuring up my world.

He spoke to my mother and said: 'Why don't you let Sarah go to the dancing school that my granddaughter Jenny Nicholson goes to?' So one day I clattered up three flights of stone stairs in George Street, Manchester Square, above a shop that sold bathroom equipment, and opposite the Spanish Church, and into the De Vos School of Dancing.

There was a senior class in progress. I watched fascinated.

Necessity endeavouring to recollect the Father of Invention.

William Nicholson left innumerable little drawings about the house.
This one is still a family favourite

Teheran: Marshal Stalin, President Roosevelt and Mr Winston Churchill,
with a group including Harry Hopkins, Molotov,
Averell Harriman, Anthony Eden and Sarah Churchill

Apart from the undeniable skill needed for the exhausting exercises, it was the expression on the faces of each of the dancers which caught my imagination. There was a serenity and isolation in these faces. Suddenly I wanted to cry. I was so sure I had found the answer to what I was looking for.

I was to dance at this school for nearly five hours a day for the next two years. At first I was so shy and awkward that I had to have private lessons. I naturally had to be in a very simple class, the average age of which was about ten. I was nineteen and felt enormous, lumbering about with these smaller pupils. It was a comprehensive training: ballet, modern, tap, even elementary acrobatics. I loved every aching moment.

I am sure these two years of hard work gave me the stamina and health I have enjoyed for most of my life, but dancing requires far more than physical ability. The body, the hands, the face are all acting, and the co-ordination when achieved is thrilling. A perfectly executed double or treble pirouette would leave me in the air for hours!

Part of the curriculum of the school as you progressed was to be sent to auditions. It was invaluable experience in conquering nerves and being able to follow directions quickly. The first time I was backstage I felt no shyness, only the tingling nerves of anticipation.

One day Miss Audrey De Vos told me that Mr C. B. Cochran was holding auditions for his new revue *Follow the Sun*. 'This would be just right for you, Sarah,' she said. 'He takes a very great interest in all his Young Ladies, and if you get the job he will teach you a great deal and help you find yourself in the theatre.'

There was to be a preliminary interview. I entered the

office of C.B. as he was called, and I liked him immediately; a fatherly, rubicund figure with merry, twinkling eyes.

He looked up from the card which had been handed to him. His first question was shattering: 'Does your father know you are here?'

I felt a sting of indignation but let it subside and replied, 'No.' Then he said, 'I am sorry but until I know that he will give his permission I cannot audition you.'

I felt crushed but went home and duly reported what had happened. Without delay my father wrote to Mr Cochran saying I had studied with perseverance and application for the last two years, it was unquestionably a burning desire of mine to be in the theatre, and he would be grateful if I could be given a serious audition, after which would Mr Cochran inform him as to the possibilities of a respectable future for me in this profession.

A few days later I had a solo audition on the stage of the Palace Theatre between the matinée and the evening show. I remember to this day the slightly stale but warm human air that crept over from the auditorium on to the stage. The green EXIT, and LADIES and GENTLEMEN signs, seen upside down as I did my elementary acrobatics, fascinated me, also the sharp rake of the stage and the dark void and silence except for a piano tinkling too far away in the pit; a disembodied voice from the darkened stalls saying. 'Thank you, could you show us another dance, please?'

I could and I did. Then it was over. The lights went up. Mr Cochran got up out of his seat and walking to the orchestra pit said, 'I would like you to be one of my Young Ladies. See the stage manager, Mr Collins. He will tell you when to report.'

I walked out of that theatre feeling an inch taller. Suddenly life had a meaning. Mourning and melancholic poetry were over. The adventure had started at last. Love could wait ... or so I thought ... but it was in this show that I met Vic Oliver who was the star, and within a few weeks our attachment was clear.

Everyone from the call-boy to C.B. himself was to give me advice and tell me not to take this affection seriously. Even Mrs Cochran was induced to invite me to tea to discourage me from the folly of any serious commitment. She poured out the tea in an abstracted way and wandered vaguely about the room. Suddenly she plucked up courage: 'Cocky is most distressed at the news that you might marry Vic. You are so young. At the beginning of your career. Life is so long.' I felt she had memorized these lines. 'My dear,' she said, 'he is eighteen years older than you, and has been married twice before. You are so young, so inexperienced. . . .'

Her voice trailed away. Silence filled the room. I could not think of anything helpful to say. I was so sorry for her in her embarrassment that I almost wanted to join in and help her with her arguments.

Suddenly she smiled and said: 'Of course I ran away from home to marry Cocky and have never regretted it.' I bade her a smiling farewell.

The only thing that really weighed on me was the effect that my decision might have on the relations between my parents and myself, which had hitherto been cloudless and happy.

One day my father called me into his room at Morpeth Mansions, our London home at that time. He was looking

51

very serious. I sat down at his bidding. He spoke to me for about half an hour. He pointed out every conceivable reason why he feared my projected marriage. I could not really disagree with him, I completely saw his point of view; a point of view any parent might voice.

He even asked: was I not betraying my own dedication to the work I had already struggled so hard for, by marrying so soon? I looked at him helplessly and speechlessly. When he finished there was a long, heavy silence.

He gazed at me with those extraordinary eyes, capable of so many expressions of subtlety and passion; eyes, as someone once remarked, that not only looked but saw deep into the human soul.

I said nothing. There was nothing I could say. Suddenly he sprang up and from his desk he picked up his British passport. Holding it dramatically in front of me he said: 'One thing I ask of you, one promise, do not marry him until he is an American citizen.' Vic was an Austrian and although he had lived some fifteen years in America he had never bothered to change his nationality. 'For if he does not take American citizenship,' my father continued, 'in three years' time you will be married to the enemy – and I will not be able to protect you once you have lost this,' and he tapped the British passport again.

This gesture brought vividly to my mind the peril in which I would place Vic as well as myself, if indeed we married before he was an American citizen.

If through the happy excitement of my entry into the theatre and the discovery of my talented and fascinating companion, I had forgotten momentarily the warnings I had heard throughout my childhood, in an instant they were once again there. I did not doubt my father's prophetic insight and I gave him my word.

Vic had to leave for America for business reasons. Some months later I followed. My family were still opposed and Randolph, who as a journalist was to cover the imminent American presidential elections, was to make a last-minute appeal as a brother, or at any rate to be at my side.

I left a day and a half before him on the *Bremen*. He caught the *Queen Mary*. For the newspapers it became a race between him and me, to see who would get to New York first.

It had never occurred to me that my decision could be of interest to the outside world. It was a rough crossing all the way. One day out from New York, we had to heave-to owing to a hurricane warning. I had hardly ever travelled unaccompanied even though I was nearly twenty-one. Certainly I had never had to make any serious decisions or fall back on myself for resourcefulness. All the emotional upheaval of my painful decision, and my first contact with publicity seemed suddenly part of the storm around us.

There was no turning back. I gazed awe-stricken at the mountainous waves. This boiling sea was fact, not imagination. From now on life would be fact as hard and sometimes as overwhelming.

A childhood rhyme crept through my mind as I gazed hypnotized at the sea: 'It's no use calling out for nurse, it only makes the matter worse.'

No retreat was possible, not that I wanted it. I felt elated, but the thought did cross my mind that we might never get to New York. Here at the beginning, the adventure might abruptly stop. Perhaps some god had sent the storm to punish me. 'I hardly think so,' I seemed suddenly to hear my father's voice. That made me laugh.

On my knees trying to pack my suitcases in the lurching, heaving ship, I firmly shut out all gloomy thoughts. But loneliness that should have been only a childhood phase, took a step closer, never ever quite to recede.

The *Bremen* was a German ship. Already at the end of 1936 the crew's attitude towards the British passengers, though correct, was far from friendly. On board there are always gala nights. These gala nights mainly took the form of some twenty or thirty sailors arriving in the main ball-room immaculately dressed and singing lustily and extremely well *Deutschland Uber Alles* . . . and other stimulating songs. I wondered perhaps if my father's warning had made me more sensitive to this very definitely chilling spectacle, but I found that other British and Americans on board had the same impression, including Nancy Astor and Lord Lothian, later the British Ambassador to Washington.

By now of course, everyone knew my story. Messages between Randolph and myself had sped between the ships. Everyone was extremely kind, and it was Lady Astor who, on arrival, arranged to gather the press together in one place and introduce me formally to the land of my grandmother, Jennie Jerome.

On arrival I was pestered by a strange lawyer, who informed me that I could be smuggled off the ship disguised as my lady's maid. Apart from the fact that I didn't have a lady's maid, I somehow felt that this would not be a correct method of entry into America, and was grateful to Lady Astor for championing my decision.

Randolph arrived the next day and I met him. I have

always been devoted to him and it was a comfort in the varying pandemoniums that followed to have him there. As soon as he knew I was all right he went about his business of covering the elections and I went about mine.

I joined Vic in his road show and in the couple of months that followed, I learned what life was like for a four-shows-a-day performer in vaudeville. Bit by bit things were sorted out. Vic became an American citizen, and with my parents' blessing we were married on Christmas Eve 1936 in New York.

RANDOLPH had been a support in those days. I thought of him now, walking ahead of us with the other men of our family. We couldn't see them because of the coachmen on their elevated seat in front of us. I thought of Randolph's devotion to my father and of his courage in all aspects of his life, and I remembered the times during the war when together we had been lucky enough to be with my father on several of the occasions when his task was at its most gigantic.

My war service, for varying reasons, did not start until October 1941. The most important of these reasons was that my husband was an American citizen and was continually being warned to return to the United States. This placed both him and me in a bitter predicament since if he did go, I, as his wife, should go with him. I can never be grateful enough that he decided to stay, knowing the sorrow he would have caused me if he had asked me to leave Britain at that time.

The difficulty of his decision could have been in no way

lessened by the fact that we both felt we were nearing the end of our road together. He stayed in Britain throughout the war and entertained the Forces and people in Britain with the radio show *Hi Gang*, in company with two other famous Americans, Bebe Daniels and Ben Lyon.

I had then to decide what I would do. I chose the WAAF, and asked my father one favour only – to see that I could get in as quickly as possible. Instead of the normal three to four weeks delay, I was in within a week.

The next problem was the choice of a job. They wanted me to be in administration, but I shrank from this. I am not very good at giving orders, so I was allowed to train as a photographic interpreter. It was a fascinating job, which fully occupied my mind during the long four years, even though I found the sedentary part of the job irksome and often wished I was driving a car, or dispensing buns and tea.

One day early in November of 1943 I was summoned to the commanding officer and told by him that leave of absence was to be granted to me so that I could accompany my father on an important journey.

The RAF station at Medmenham was quite near to Chequers and whenever I had forty-eight hours' leave it was quite easy for me to get over there. I hurried there now, and my father told me that a conference between the President of the United States, Stalin and himself had been arranged at Teheran, that the President despite his health and physical handicap was making the long journey and that Stalin had finally been lured from his lair. My father and the President were to meet in Cairo before the conference in Teheran. I was to accompany my father as one of his aides-de-camp ... I walked on air.

At six o'clock on November 12th, with the light failing and the sky overcast, we drew alongside a quay at Plymouth where a blue-grey tender waited to take us to the battle-cruiser *Renown*. My father was not feeling well, owing to the many injections he had had, and was lying down. So Admiral Cunningham, Ambassador Winant, General Ismay, my brother Randolph, and myself went on in the first tender. If you have ever tried boarding a battleship from a tender in a swell, you will remember it is no easy thing.

'You first, Mrs Oliver,' said Admiral Cunningham briskly, as we arrived.

I gazed helplessly up at the steel monster, now close – now far away. I thought: if I don't move we shall never get to the conference. I braced myself and prepared to leap, scramble or clutch anything that came to hand.

'Wait for it, wait for it!' came the voice of Cunningham behind me. I waited. It seemed hours but I suppose it was only a matter of seconds. I caught the rising swell and with the aid of a judicious prod in the back I reached the gang-plank and was aboard the *Renown*.

All our complement got safely aboard, although Charles Wilson (now Lord Moran) did have a nasty fall getting into the tender which brought my father and the rest of our party. When I heard of his misfortune the next day I gave him a look of sympathy. One of my father's joys on these trips was to pretend to look after Charles Wilson. The first day out there was a horrid swell, and only half of our distinguished company surfaced for breakfast. I faced and ate a fried egg with bacon, but had to admit that I did it with more concentration than enjoyment.

After a night's sleep my father was feeling much better,

and lunch saw a full and determined complement of the entourage. Lord Moran had a hard tussle and when luncheon was over, but not until, he excused himself. My father arose solicitously from the table and accompanied him to the door, advising him what to do and what not to do, delaying his departure yet another agonizing ten minutes. My father was fond of him, and took all his pills most obediently, despite the fact that he often remarked that 'Charles when ill refuses his own drugs with a sad air of inside knowledge'.

It was dark when we anchored at Gibraltar. The Rock rose from the sea in solitary splendour, surrounded by a necklace of lights, the first I had seen since the blackout had begun in 1939.

My duties were mainly to see, along with others, to my father's comfort and wishes, to relay messages, and to drape myself silently along with the coat racks in the ante-chambers of the conference rooms with other ADCs assigned to similar duties. I did not have any 'ideas above my station'.

We stopped at Gibraltar only long enough to pick up Harold Macmillan, who was the Minister Resident in Algeria. It was a wonderful night, one night after full moon: the *Renown* never looked more magnificent. As I stood on her moon-silvered decks, A and B turrets and then the bridge rose in grand echelon to the stars. Port, starboard, for'ard and aft the black shapes of our escorts glided. The *London*, at our stern, was so close it seemed you could almost pat her nose.

On these long journeys my father would stay much in bed, working. For relaxation he played bezique with Randolph for many hours. He was not feeling at all well throughout the sea voyage, but when he appeared at dinner you would not have known it.

We arrived at Malta on November 17th at about 6 p.m. Generals Eisenhower and Alexander were there to greet my father. Before dinner that night with General Gort, the Governor of Malta, my father on behalf of the King decorated General Eisenhower and General Alexander with the North Africa Ribbon, with the numerals 1 and 8 upon it, which represented the two victorious armies of that campaign. They are the only two allowed to wear both figures on the one ribbon. They were surprised and delighted.

My father's health had not improved – a cold had set in, so, sensible as always, he went to bed and read a book about Pitt, which my mother had sent him and which kept him happy for hours. Apart from the dinner with General Gort, he only got up for a Staff Conference and for a tour of the battered docks on the day of our departure.

We sailed at midnight for Alexandria, and I was sad to think that this part of the trip was nearly over.

Mary had accompanied my parents on a trip the year before to the Quebec Conference. She had joined the ATS, serving with a mixed anti-aircraft battery. Her company had to deal with the 'scalded cat' raids on London – and, of course, with the flying bombs – and she spent many nights standing with her girls in an open pit during raids. On the return journey from Quebec to England they travelled aboard the *Renown*. Although on one occasion she was almost washed overboard by an immense wave, she felt the same as I did about the Navy. There did not appear to be anything they would not do to keep us happy, and always they treated us with delightful courtesy.

On my journey in the *Renown* they were, as usual, anxious to keep me amused. As we neared the port of Alexandria, one of the officers asked me if I would like to say a few words to the 'boys upstairs'.

High above us in the pale blue air one could see our RAF escort circling protectively. I didn't like to refuse although I was quite nervous about the whole thing and had to admit that this strictly chair-borne officer had never spoken over an RT system. The words 'over and out' and 'Roger' came to my mind, but beyond that I found it difficult to think of anything to say. 'Hello, up there!' seemed inadequate. However, rising to the moment as I thought, I said, 'Hello would you like to come and beat us up?'

The air crackled with static or something: 'Would we like to what?' – 'Come and beat us up.' – 'Who's that speaking?' – 'Sarah,' I replied, my eyes gazing up at their orderly circle above our heads.

Suddenly one and then all of them, peeled away, diving down steadily towards us. The young officer dived for the intercom: 'Gun control,' he shouted, 'the following beat-up is official, for God's sake hold your fire.' The diving planes would obviously be picked up on the ship's radar. My heart rose in my mouth at the realization of the enormity of what I had done. Down they came.

Admiral Cunningham was on the bridge, as was my father, watching the navigator bringing the great ship into port, steering clear of half-submerged wrecks. Level with the eyes of everyone on the bridge the Spitfires shot by them, dipping to almost sea level, when with an enormous roar, they soared back into the sky. It was magnificent, but I was never so glad as when it was over, and I kept out of sight until we docked. Nothing was said until at the airport we met Group Captain Max Aitken, Lord Beaverbrook's son, whose squadron it was.

'So it was you,' he said sternly. 'I'm afraid so,' I said, and crawled into the plane for Cairo.

The arrangements in Cairo were splendid. We lived in the palatial villa of Mr R. G. Casey, Minister of State Resident in the Middle East. The following morning the President arrived. My father, Commander 'Tommy' Thompson (his personal assistant) and myself paid him a formal visit. This was my first meeting with him; I found him immensely impressive. One knew, of course, of his physical handicap, but after two minutes one never thought of it again. He was a vivid personality with a disarming air of simplicity. A great warmth emanated from him.

One day after lunch with the President, my father called me aside and said, 'Arrange a car. I want to go and have a look at the Sphinx and the Pyramids. I want to see how close you can get in a car, because if it is possible I want to take the President, but I don't want to raise his hopes if we can't get close enough.'

We set out on our reconnaissance together. We found it was possible to get quite close, so we drove straight back and my father bounded into the room and said: 'Mr President, you simply must come and see the Sphinx and Pyramids. I've arranged it all.'

Such was my father's enthusiasm that the President leaned forward on the arms of his chair and seemed about to rise, when he remembered that he could not and sank back again. It was a painful moment. My father turned abruptly away and called over his shoulder: 'We'll wait for you in the car.' Outside in the shimmering sun, I saw that his eyes were bright with tears. 'I love that man,' he said simply. The visit to the Pyramids was a great success.

The night before we left for Teheran, my father was in terrific spirits at dinner, and despite a husky, tired voice he talked from 8.30 until 1.30 a.m. He talked everyone into the ground except Anthony Eden. Mountbatten went to sleep on a sofa, and I did not know how to keep my eyes open.

On the way home that night my father talked lovingly about my mother and indulged himself with the thought of sending planes to get her, although he knew he could not. Then he fell silent and presently said, 'War is a game played with a smiling face, but do you think there is laughter in my heart? We travel in style and round us there is great luxury and seeming security, but I never forget the man at the front, the bitter struggles, and the fact that men are dying in the air, on the land, and at sea.'

The next morning, November 27th, we left at 8.30 for Teheran. My father's voice was bad, but as he strode on board the plane he said: 'Now for the high jump.' He settled himself calmly into his seat and then continued: 'We shall be crossing four great rivers, the Tigris, the Euphrates, Jordan, and Nile, and the wilderness and the mountains. There will be nowhere, should we feel tired, that we could put our feet down to rest.' I tingled with excitement.

It was indeed a wonderful flight over the rocky desert, then over the desolate range of the Persian mountains, for the most part sepia coloured, but every now and then slashed with a red or aquamarine seam of colour.

I didn't know until we were on the plane that Stalin had

'jumped the gun'. He had already arrived in Teheran some twenty-four hours before the Americans and our party, and was safely ensconced in his embassy. It was not thought by any of us that this was a smart thing to do. With his presence there, it was quite obvious that a conference was afoot, and therefore plenty of time had been given for the Germans to send agents in.

The security arrangements in Teheran seemed to us a little bizarre. The President arrived forty-five minutes before us, as arranged. I do not know what his trip into the city was like, but ours was spine-chilling. We crawled through streets thronged with people, our route picked out by the white horses of the Persian Cavalry. Anyone could have shot my father at point blank range or just dropped a nice little grenade into our laps. We were in a car alone with Mr Bullard, later Sir Reader Bullard, the British Minister; the atmosphere was tense. I scanned the swarthy, often handsome, but dead-pan faces of the crowds. Behind us there followed a Jeep, full to capacity with soldiers with rifles, but they had the hood up.

My father noticed this and remarked: 'If anything should happen, I don't see what they could do. Inevitably they must be greatly impeded. I think in future it will be better for them while on duties of this nature to ride in an open Jeep. Not, of course,' he added tersely, 'that they could do anything to save us, but at least it would save them the embarrassment of not being able to do anything at all.'

At one point we were caught in a traffic block and were stationary for all of three minutes. The crowd pressed around the car. I put my hand on his knee lightly and as lightly he covered my hand with his. He grinned at the

64

Yalta: President Roosevelt and Mr Winston Churchill,
with their daughters Mrs Anna Boettiger and Sarah Churchill

Sarah Churchill

crowd, which as he says in his own account 'for the most part grinned back'. We learned later that the Shah had announced that he would take a state drive through Teheran about the time of the arrival of the President and my father: but nobody thought of telling us this.

We arrived at a cold and cheerless Legation, and the Americans wanted to have talks with my father at once, but this, Lord Moran and the rest of us felt, was most unwise. Ambassador Winant stepped in firmly and persuaded his fellow Americans to leave him alone by saying: 'If you don't know what you are going to say tomorrow, it's too late anyway.'

My father, pale and morose, rather like an actor with first-night nerves, got into bed surrounded by hot-water bottles, and as he sometimes did on these occasions, picked up a book as far as possible removed from the present day – I think it was *Oliver Twist* – and read solidly until midnight.

In the morning, the voice was back with familiar resonance and strength, and the conference began.

This was the conference at which, among other things, 'Overlord', the invasion of France, was planned. It was the first meeting of all the three leaders. Everyone was relieved and surprised at the genuinely mutual facility of expression between the three of so vastly different temperaments.

On November 30th, my father's sixty-ninth birthday, he gave a never-to-be-forgotten party. Stalin, a frightening figure with his slit, bear eyes, was in jovial mood. Specks of light danced in his eyes like cold sunshine on dark waters. He pounced on every remark with a dry and often sly humour.

The party was a glittering affair. The three interpreters

rose I felt, to histrionic heights. It wasn't just a matter of interpreting serious proposals, but of translating the nature of the different senses of humour which flashed between the three. Toasts were proposed and answered all through the long banquet. I think this is a very agreeable idea instead of the numerous and generally endless speeches at the conclusion of a dinner. Between the courses anyone who felt inclined would spring up and propose a toast. Then, to the accompaniment of 'Da, da' and 'Hear, hear' the toaster would walk round and clink glasses with the toastee.

At one point, to my very great surprise, my health was proposed by the President. Stalin rose and walked slowly round the table to me. We clinked glasses and bowed to each other. I hesitated a fraction, then walked round the table to the President and thanked him, and as we touched glasses he said: 'I would have come to you, my dear, but I cannot.'

Randolph had been able to join us for this occasion, but he was seated far away from me. I wished, despite the distinguished companions by my side, I had been next to him on this never-to-be-forgotten evening.

When after four high-tensioned days the conference was over, there was a feeling of genuine elation shared by all three parties, of 'mission completed'. We flew back to Cairo knowing that the high jump had been cleared, and with feet to spare. Turtle soup and champagne over Baghdad had indeed the sweet taste of success.

When we got back to Cairo everyone, though still elated, felt exhausted. Randolph and the President's son-in-law, Major Boettiger, were sent off to get the Turkish delegation then in Cairo. It had been my father's hope that Turkey would enter the war, but the Turks were still greatly impressed by the German military machine and they shivered on the brink for a few months, so for the time being at least they decided to maintain their neutrality.

Although, therefore, the talks were cautious and unrewarding, my father had cordial relations with President Inonu. When I went to say good night to him after their departure, and to tuck his mosquito net round him, I found him giggling quietly to himself. When I inquired the reason he said 'The President of the Turks kissed me – twice. The trouble with me is that I am irresistible,' and with that fell into a contented sleep.

It was over – goodbyes were said. Shortly after midnight on December 11th, we clambered aboard our York. Our first stop was Tunis: there I was to fly on to England to return to my more prosaic duties. My father wanted to go to Italy to visit the headquarters of General Alexander and General Montgomery.

The flight to Tunis was uneventful, but as we were circling to land early in the morning, our wheels already down, suddenly the heavy York heaved itself up into the sky again, retracting its undercarriage rapidly. We all looked at each other in surprise. The pilot sent us a message that he had received warning signals not to land, so we landed on an operational airfield some forty miles away.

We climbed out and gazed about the somewhat desolate scene. After the hot plane it was cold, but the luggage was unloaded and my father sat on his official boxes, while a mean little breeze whipped around. I believe that this is where, in his exhausted condition, the pneumonia soon to attack found its chance.

There were a few aircraft men working on their Beau-fighters drawn up in a nearby line. At first they took little notice of the motley crowd that had tumbled out sleepy-eyed from the York, but I noticed their eyes become riveted on the solitary figure sitting humped up in the middle of their field. Whispers spread among them, and one by one they left their aircraft and came and stared at him. They were probably prepared for many things to fall out of the sky, but not the Prime Minister!

News came that the signal had been a mistake after all, and since it would take over an hour to get cars to us, General Eisenhower, who was waiting for us, suggested that we get back in the plane and return. This we did with alacrity; we waved goodbye to the airmen and took off, and in ten minutes were safely down on our appointed field.

My father rode with General Eisenhower to the small villa known as the Little White House, which was one of the general's temporary HQs. He confessed to him that he was feeling quite exceptionally tired, and that he simply could not go any further and must rest for a few days. General Eisenhower immediately did what he could to make the small villa comfortable for our rather large contingent.

My father got into bed and fell into a deep sleep, too exhausted even to ask for his papers. Lord Moran became very concerned. As we walked up and down the long, pleasant room overlooking the Mediterranean he confided to me: 'He is sickening for something, but I do not know what.'

All that day my father slept. Signals were sent out for doctors, specialists and nurses. Speedily they winged their way to us through the night. I saw Lord Moran's increasing concern, and I stayed anxiously in my father's room watching him sleep. Once he opened his eyes, and must have caught my troubled look before I had time to mask it. He looked at me without speaking for a moment, then said: 'Don't worry, it doesn't matter if I die now, the plans of victory have been laid, it is only a matter of time,' and fell into a deep sleep once more.

When he next woke his temperature was up, but at the foot of his bed were the doctors and nurses, armed with powerful drugs, summoned by Lord Moran's foresight, to stamp out immediately the pneumonia which had now clearly shown its hand. The forty-eight hours' rest had given him the strength to suffer and survive this short but sharp attack.

WE were now approaching the Law Courts, and still there were people crowding the pavements. I thought about English Common Law and how American law is to a very great degree founded on the principles we have hammered out sorely through the years. I remembered hearing of the libel action my father felt it necessary to bring against Lord Alfred Douglas after the Battle of Jutland in 1915. And of the other case when, as Home Secretary, he had to advise George V to fight, at once and quickly, the criminal libel that could have threatened the Monarchy, his marriage and his happiness at the beginning of his reign.

I turned and looked at my mother, who must have suffered acutely through so many crises and decisions. She was so still – the stillest of all. Mary and I exchanged a glance. 'I thought there was going to be music,' my mother said. 'There is, but we can't hear it,' we replied almost in unison. Only the drums and the distant guns and the horses' hooves and our gently creaking carriage ... The noise reminded me of the sea, of boats that sigh and creak ... a boat had carried some of our forefathers long ago to a far-off land . . . to Plymouth . . . Plymouth Rock . . . Jennie . . . vibrant Jennie Jerome whose blood we have in our veins. All through his life my father had longed to link this England with his motherland, and how passionately he fought to bring about the unity of English-speaking people. After Suez he had worked with determination and great success for the improvement of Anglo-American relations. He did this in a way no one else could and his private diplomacy was enormously effective. It was one of the truly great services he rendered after his retirement.

Fleet Street reminded me of his start in journalism. By the standards of that day he was not a rich man – he had to earn his bread and butter, and labour to support his family and to educate his children by the fruits of his pen. A jingle ran through my mind, written of him during the Boer war:

> *You've heard of Winston Churchill;*
> *This is all I need to say*
> *He's the latest and the greatest*
> *Correspondent of the day.*

I thought of Randolph's son, the young Winston, walking beside his father, and remembered how he too was following steadfastly in the family tradition.

'War is a game played with a smiling face – but do you think there is laughter in my heart?' My father had said this to me on one of our drives together during the journey to Teheran; and I was to learn this could apply to life also. I was to have ample evidence of this at another time, when I went with him to Yalta.

I was still at the RAF station at Medmenham in January 1945 when one afternoon I received a message which told me that I was to accompany my father on another journey. As before, secrecy and excitement prevailed. There was the last-minute rush for prosaic but necessary things like my laundry. I had to invent another story to explain to my friends my sudden departure.

A second conference had been arranged between the Big Three – Roosevelt, Stalin and my father – and I learned we would be flying to Malta to await the President's arrival.

At about 9.30 on a bitter night, January 29th, our party clambered aboard a Skymaster which had been given to us by the President and had been fitted out by the RAF. It was extremely comfortable and seemed as silent as a ghost. It had a specially designed interior so that emergency conferences could be held.

Though my father had an amazing constitution the heavy injections before these trips sometimes made him feel ill, and once again he was to start out on a journey not feeling his best. At first the plane was very cold, so all the heat was turned on and in a few minutes we were screaming for air. My father asked for a thermometer. His temperature was up and it subsequently rose to 102° during the night. My heart sank and I thought, 'Oh, Lord, here we go again,' but there was nothing to do but settle down. Nobody slept much.

The time of our departure from London had been advanced owing to a weather report of snow, and 'Tommy' Thompson, my father's indispensable wartime personal assistant, had sent a message asking that any reception at Malta should be cancelled, as we would now be arriving uncomfortably early, and my father would want to sleep on in the grounded plane. As far as Tommy knew, this message had been relayed, but when we landed at Malta at about 4.30 a.m., we found, to our horror, that everything but massed bands was waiting to greet us. The tarmac was laced with gold braid. Something had obviously gone wrong and some very angry top brass rumbled off back to their beds. Tommy faced the flood of their anger stoically and crawled back into the Skymaster.

I found it impossible to sleep in the silence of the grounded aircraft, where every rustle and sigh could be heard, so I dressed in my bunk – a feat to test any contortionist. Somehow the long hours crept by. I pulled back the blackout from my window and saw the sunrise over the hangars of the airfield. The pale blue sky grew warmer and the grass was emerald green. There was no snow.

My father's temperature had dropped to 101° in the morning, but he was miserable and thought he might be 'in' for something. Sawyers, his valet, a paragon of devotion, muttered consolingly to me, 'He's always like this after those pills.' I meditated on this profound statement and passed it on to my father who grunted and said, 'True.'

'It is a pretty powerful drug,' I continued, 'and, as Sawyers says, you always have a strong reaction to it.' Lord Moran, despite the comment on his drugs, remained calm, but still thought it wise for my father to see a specialist before he left the aircraft.

It remained 'touch and go' for a few hours whether it would not be better for him to go to the hospital instead of to the harbour of Valetta, where HMS *Orion* was waiting to accommodate us.

When we finally boarded the *Orion*, the bed in my father's cabin was the wrong way round. I have never quite understood why one way was right and another wrong, as I didn't think my father had any feelings about facing Mecca, but anyway Sawyers knew all about it and carefully redesigned his cabin.

Bed, hot water bottles – and my father fell asleep. We lunched without him, and when late in the afternoon Lord Moran decided to wake him his temperature was down. He then immediately set to work. The Governor of Malta, General Gort, Field-Marshal Sir Alan Brooke, Field-Marshal Sir Harold Alexander and Anthony Eden arrived in quick succession; Anthony and Alexander Cadogan of the Foreign Office, with Averell Harriman came back for dinner.

The pre-conference talks were not to let up until our departure for Yalta in the early hours of February 3rd.

Driving with him one or two nights later to have dinner with General Gort, and seeing him well and in good fettle, I told him that I would be finishing a letter to my mother that night. Charles had sent his report to her as to the state of his health, and I, of course, would be sending her mine – would he perhaps like to add something himself?

'Indeed I would,' he replied. 'Tell her my temperature's down, my tummy-ache gone. My functions have resumed their norm – in fact I'm in the best of form.'

During our stay in Malta while we were waiting for the President, dramatic telegrams kept coming in from Lord Ismay's right-hand woman, Joan Bright, about the conditions at Yalta. Two bathrooms for thirty people! Sixteen American colonels in one room! Yalta was six hours from Saki airfield in the Crimea, and three hours from the

SS *Franconia*, the ship that was waiting in the port of Sebastopol to be used as a communication centre. Obviously it was impracticable, owing to the distance, for the ship to be used to house any member of the conference.

Averell Harriman came in for most of the blame. Green with pain from a twisted ankle, he just murmured: 'It was there, or two worse places.'

Anyway, since the Russians had been told that the complement of each party would be thirty-five, and that our numbers now totalled over five hundred souls, nothing more could be done.

My father had cabled previously to the President: 'No more let us falter! From Malta to Yalta! Let nobody alter.' He now enlarged upon this – as the news from Joan kept coming in: 'No more let us alter or falter or palter. From Malta to Yalta, and Yalta to Malta.'

About mid-morning on February 2nd, the President arrived aboard the USS *Quincy* which steamed into Valetta Harbour. It was a great moment and a thrilling sight. The sailors of both ships lined the rails, and everyone turned out on deck. The President was seated in a chair on the bridge of the *Quincy*. The two friends waved to each other. The Maltese thronged the roof-tops. *God Save the King* and the *Star-Spangled Banner* were played and the ships passed so close that it was easy to recognize familiar faces. The person, however, who seemed to know most people on the President's ship was Sawyers, who bowed and waved gracefully in acknowledgement continuously. The rest of us stood to attention.

Very soon afterwards we paid a formal call on the President. We found him sitting in the sun with his daughter,

Anna Boettiger. I had warm feelings for the President, and I hope I hid my shock at the terrible change in him since I had last seen him at the Teheran conference. It was quite obvious that he was a very sick man; the bright charm and the brave, expansive heart were there, but his appearance gravely distressed my father and, indeed, everyone.

It is well known now that the mood of this conference was to be very different from the one at Teheran the year before. Perhaps due to the President's frailness there was no longer quite the intimate contact that had existed before. He was very much surrounded by officials of his State Department. My father and all the British party felt a withdrawing of the former easy understanding which, in spite of many disagreements, had existed between the two leaders.

On the eve of our departure for Yalta, news came in that one of our Yorks had crash-landed off the Mediterranean island of Lampedusa and that thirteen out of nineteen were lost, including three brilliant young men all specially briefed for the conference. Everyone was shocked and grieved, and it was in a serious and sombre mood that we set out on the journey.

We got into our separate planes at 3.30 a.m. on February 3rd, and flew off to Saki, where we arrived at about 10.30 the same morning. We touched down before the President, but my father waited for him before greeting Molotov and Vyshinsky. There was a miniature parade. The President, in a car, and my father walking by its side, together inspected the guard of honour. Then we got into our cars and the long convoy took off for the journey to Yalta. How the President endured that endless and tiring drive I cannot imagine.

For the first two hours the roads were bad and we had to crawl at about twenty miles an hour over bumpy, slushy tracks, through a countryside as black as a soul in despair. I sat with my father in the back of the car. 'This drive will waste a whole day and another precious one on the way back,' he exclaimed. After what seemed an eternity he asked how long we had been going. I replied, 'About an hour.' 'God,' he said, 'five hours more of this!'

However, after two and a half hours we reached the mountains and the countryside improved. Characteristically my father was able to move himself out of a gloomy mood by suddenly taking an interest in his surroundings. But there was no sign of the rest-house about which we had been told. The whole hundred miles of the road was lined every two hundred yards with Red Army men and girls who sprang to salute.

On and on we went; still no rest-house, so we stopped and ate a stale ham sandwich and had a swig of some very good brandy. When at last hope had nearly died, the convoy halted. We were at the rest-house.

We clambered out for what we thought would be a short pause and were led into a room stacked with food and wine. And there, too, was a smiling Molotov. The Americans would not stop. They had decided to hurry on. The Russians looked very disappointed until my father and I fell on the food and showed by our appetites our appreciation of this thoughtful gesture. It was a delightful occasion. The only Russians who were present were Molotov, Vyshinsky, Gusov, and little Pavlov the interpreter, who should have been an actor and was decidedly a Chekhovian character.

How we regretted our stale ham sandwich, which just

took the edge off our appetites! After about one and a half hours we set off again. There was still another two hours to go, but these passed, for me at least, most enjoyably. My father, relaxed and fortified, recited for an hour from *Childe Harold* by Byron and then had about thirty minutes' sleep. Darkness fell, but our headlamps picked out our sentinels still lining their road. At long, long last, eight hours from the start of the drive, we arrived at Yalta.

The ablution position was almost as grim as Joan Bright had said, but the villa was warm and light and Russian hospitality once again left little to be desired. My father insisted that I should share his bathroom, but we were told that any spectator in the corridors of the other villas at about 7.30 a.m. would have seen three field-marshals queueing for a bucket.

Our villa, the Vorontzov palace, was quite a fantastic affair. It was like a Scottish baronial hall inside and a Swiss chalet with a mosque attached outside. It had apparently been a museum before the war and as the Germans had used it as their headquarters, it was less knocked about than the other buildings in the neighbourhood, which all showed signs of looting.

Though the problems were tougher this conference did not seem as hard physically as Teheran the year before. The Big Three met at four in the afternoon when they would have, as my father put it, a 'whacking' session of four to five hours and then part, returning to their 'separate lairs'.

For the most part my father dined alone at the Vorontzov villa with just Anthony Eden and myself. It was during these evenings that sometimes the mask fell from their faces and I learned something of their problems. I saw their grave concern. Stalin was out to woo the Americans, and the Americans were there to be wooed. Here, while they ate almost in silence, I saw the reality of what those two men had to face.

Dinner over I would take my leave of them while they went to their separate rooms to rest and wait until the arrival of the Diplomatic Bag, which we, the family, called the 'Pouch', containing the latest confidential despatches from London. This unfortunately did not reach them until about midnight, which meant at least another two hours of reading before they could get to sleep.

If the Pouch was very late, my father would naturally sleep late and there wasn't time for breakfast, work, and lunch and a little sleep before the 'do' at four in the afternoon, so he would just have a meal at 11.30 a.m. and then nothing until 9 o'clock in the evening. This seemed to those concerned a very long time, but I was always amazed at the careful planning of his time of rest and necessary nutriment so he was always at his peak physically when the Big Show started at 4 o'clock.

Both Anna Boettiger and Kathleen Harriman were charming and highly intelligent companions, and during the day we would often go about together. One day we decided to visit Sebastopol. It was a two and a half hour drive over grand but gloomy country.

Sebastopol was a terrible sight. We didn't see one house that had not been shattered, yet still the people lived there and strangely enough they did not look too poverty stricken or hungry. Our guide was a Russian sailor who showed us around the town as though there were no ruins at all.

'This,' he said with pride, 'is a very beautiful church.'

We looked at a scarred shell and nodded. 'Oh, yes,' he said, 'Sebastopol is a beautiful city.' He took us to vanished monument after vanished monument. 'This is the Sports Club – this square is lovely in summer.' We gazed dumbfounded at a devastated area – a square wilderness of broken trees and shell holes.

As we said goodbye he said: 'You like Sebastopol?' For a moment we didn't answer and at once his face fell. 'No? You don't like it?'

'Of course, of course,' I said. 'It's just that it makes me so sad to see it like this.'

But somehow it was the wrong thing to have said. He was disappointed. He had been seeing Sebastopol like someone who still sees a person they really love unchanged in spite of some terrible physical tragedy, but now he looked at it with our eyes and said slowly: 'We will build it up again – in five years – you'll see. You will come back to Sebastopol, my Sebastopol, and I will show you around again.' We promised that we would come back.

I described all this to my father that night at dinner and when I went to say good night to him later, he took my hand and said: 'I do not suppose that at any moment in history has the agony of the world been so great or widespread. Tonight the sun goes down on more suffering than ever before in the world.'

On February 8th, about the middle of our stay, the Russians gave one of their superb banquets at their villa. The 'Little Three', as Anna, Kathy and I were humorously called, were invited. The 'Bear' was at his most friendly. The girls were toasted and Kathy surpassed herself by answering in Russian, thanking them all for all they had

Tea in the Garden,
a portrait of her father by Sarah Churchill

done to make everyone so comfortable. They were delighted.

I sat next to twinkly-eyed Vyshinsky. I found him agreeable and easy although he could hardly speak a word of English. The food and drink proved too much for us long before half-way through, and with a wink we both of us took to 'Narzair Minerale Vode' and toyed delicately with our sucking pigs.

The head of the Ogpu was there, and with the aid of Mr Maisky, the former ambassador to London, I recited to him the only five Russian sentences I knew. I always believe in starting with practical things, and one phrase I recited was: 'Can I have a hot-water bottle, please?' to which Ogpu replied: 'I cannot believe that you need one. Surely there is enough fire in you.' It looked as if there was a future to this conversation, but at that point dinner was served and I went off to try my hot-water bottle line on Mr Vyshinsky.

I must have said it with greater emphasis for it had a very different effect on him. He said with all seriousness and not a little surprise: 'Why? are you ill?' As my Russian lessons ended at that point, I had to take to sign language and vodka to make him see that it was a joke.

February 12th, and it was over. Hopes had risen steadily during the last two days as the deadlocks seemed to have been broken, and at that time no one knew that Stalin was to falsify his promises. Warm goodbyes were said. It had been decided we should leave the following morning, easily, orderly, and quietly, but on the way back from the American villa my father suddenly felt lonely, I think, and said to me, 'Why do we stay here? Why don't we go tonight? I see no reason to stay here a minute longer. We're off.'

He sprang out of the car and, whirling into the private

office, announced to the secretaries: 'I don't know about you but I'm off. I leave in fifty minutes.' After a second's stunned silence, everyone was galvanised into activity. Trunks and large mysterious paper parcels given to us by the Russians – caviar we hoped – filled the hall. Laundry arrived back clean but damp. Naturally fifty minutes gave my father time to change our minds several more times.

'We will spend the night here after all and leave tomorrow lunchtime.' – 'We will leave tonight and go by sea.' – 'We will fly from Saki.' – 'We will go to Athens – Alexandria – Cairo – Constantinople.' – 'We will not go to any of them. We will stay on board the *Franconia* and read the newspapers.' – 'Where is the Pouch?' – 'Why hasn't it arrived?'

Sawyers on his knees, tears in his eyes, surrounded by half-packed suitcases, literally beat his breast in truly classical style and said: 'They can't do this to me.'

He put a sponge-bag into a case and then took it out. He carefully laid out the Lord Warden of the Cinque Ports suit, then changed it for the Royal Yacht Squadron suit. My father, genial and sprightly like a boy out of school, his homework done, walked from room to room saying: 'Come on, come on.'

One hour and twenty minutes later, at about 5.30 p.m., a cavalcade of cars groaning with bulging suitcases wound its way to the port of Sebastopol where the *Franconia* lay waiting to bring us back to Britain.

Quick as we had been, we were the last to leave Yalta. The President had left an hour before us, but on an orderly plan laid days before. Stalin, like some genie, just disappeared.

All the way to Sebastopol we had our sentinels.

Sebastopol at night was a revelation. From nearly every ruin, wherever four walls of one room still stood, from behind boards that filled gaps, from basements, even from piles of stones, shafts and specks of light shone and twinkled as in an undamaged city. It was incredible. They were incredible!

On board the *Franconia* I asked my father if he were tired. He was silent a moment then said: 'Strangely enough, no. Yet I have felt the weight of responsibility more than ever before and in my heart there is anxiety.' He fell silent again. Suddenly he smiled, 'I think I'll fly to Athens. Opinions are divided as to the wisdom of this move, but I shall go.' He grinned and asked me, 'Have you ever been there?' 'No,' I replied. 'Oh well, then that decides it. We shall definitely go and I shall show you the Parthenon.' And he grinned again, gaily.

I saw again my father's gallantry against heavy odds. His prophetic mind had been aware – even in the momentary hope of the Teheran Conference of 1943 – of the already disastrous involvements, obligations, and assumptions that were being made. But he was a man to take one step at a time. Teheran for him signalled the inevitable and blessed end of the war, with free men triumphant. The end of Yalta told him that free men would once again be enslaved by obtuse and interminable recriminations and by the rise of a new tyranny.

But there was nothing he could do about it. And so he turned his mind towards the next phase, and the problems it would bring to Britain. The war was nearly over, and he began to plan for peace: the Beveridge Report, demobilization, and the task of confronting the British people, exhausted and bled, with the marked change in their world position.

He was not to be the architect for this new phase. He was rejected in 1945 by the same people who had trusted him in despair. Such is democracy – and such he hoped it would always be.

WE were at Ludgate Hill now; the noise of the brakes of the carriage awoke me to the fact. During these last years the world had paid him tribute that few men in their lifetime could hope to know. This perhaps makes the younger generation think that his life, so full of achievement, was easy and that he never really came to grips with the bitterness of defeat, despair and doubt.

This was far from true; he knew exhilaration and despair to the full, but he also knew the perils of the extremes of both. What were the great controversial things which hit him as hard as his triumphs for England warmed him? What of the Dardanelles? . . . the loss of India? . . . the Irish Rebellion? . . . the delay of rearmament in the Thirties? . . . the Abdication? . . . Munich? These were all fierce moments when the British were to doubt him.

I was in the hairdressers when the news of the result of the General Election became apparent. This may seem a trivial place to be, but having voted there is really nothing much more one can do than to await the result. There was a radio playing and by the time I had emerged from the dryer it was quite evident that Labour had had an overwhelming victory.

It was an extraordinary thing, judging by the faces of the people who had voted, that this should be so. They looked stunned, rather like a child that has pressed the fire alarm bell and is somewhat confused by the promptness with which the fire engine arrives. The wives of course had voted the way their husbands had told them to. Six years under Army authority had made for a certain feeling of rebellion – not exactly rebellion, but a feeling that they had fought for their country and they subconsciously wished to express themselves against authority. Officer types – officer types were conservative types so . . . Many who voted Labour had the impression that they could vote Labour and still have Winston Churchill. This they were to learn was not to be so.

I went promptly to the Annexe where we were to have lunch and where on the wall of Captain Pym's office, instead of the operational war maps, the operational results of this election were being marked up.

My father sat at the head of the table and acknowledged the news of each result with a nod of the head, and passed no comment. As it became increasingly obvious that it was a tidal wave, his natural humour reasserted itself, superficially anyhow. We, however, could not feel quite so merry, but we allowed ourselves a certain amount of hilarity whenever there was a Liberal loss, though many of them were our friends.

We chewed our way through a lunch which was perfect for the occasion, nothing that one couldn't swallow, and practised the art of conversation. Suddenly my mother said: 'Winston, this may be a blessing in disguise.' My father looked at her and replied: 'Well, it is certainly very well disguised.'

The last week-end at Chequers was of course a sombre one. It was not so much the loss of power that he minded but the sudden loss of a job to do. Six years geared to the utmost mental as well as physical exertion, and suddenly nothing: it was a shock amounting to a shattering and unexpected blow in the solar plexus, and that blow from a friend. 'I miss the boxes,' he said (the official despatch boxes). They had become so much a part of his life. The key which opened the cabinet boxes, which had always been on his watch chain and which he had never slept without, was no longer there. There was no screech of a motor cycle coming in and the scattering of the gravel as the Pouch arrived. And as I have said, the physical shock as well as the mental, of sudden and complete cessation of work, was a hiatus he had to deal with in his body. Of course he did it. 'Eels get used to skinning,' he had often said.

The day after the election I wrote to him . . .

Darling, darling Papa,

You won't forget what you said last night about the Chartwell Colony, will you? No lovelier plot of land exists and there will be plenty of space and we could till the land and milk the cows and feed the chickens and you could have an enormous bell that you clanged when you wanted to see us, and when you did we would emerge from our little cottages and make our way down the valley. Some of us would cross the lake and we could all have an evening together and when do we really have better ones?

You were never more wonderful than last night. I am not half as good as you and Mama are about it. I am glad I went with you on one day of your great tour, I needed it for myself because I've been so hurt for you, so angry and bewildered at the violence and bitterness of the opening personal attacks on you by former colleagues, and the drive with you helps me now. Because after that day whatever convulsion has taken place I know that you are as high in their hearts as you ever were.

You know it is ironically funny, you know you were saying 'In war resolution, in peace goodwill, in victory magnanimity, in defeat defiance' well you taught me a great thing last night, in defeat humour. The other thing that has been running through my head is a bit out of my favourite prayer: 'To give and not to count the cost, to fight and not to heed the wounds, to toil and not to seek for rest, to labour and not to ask for any reward'. Well that certainly is your war record.

God bless you darling,

All my love to you and Mama.

My mother was out of Downing Street quicker than lightning. She was quite an old hand at this sort of thing and when an election took place while we were occupying a Government house, she was always fully prepared for any result and, if adverse, immediate departure.

They took a suite in Claridges for the time being, until they could find a London house, and I remember him standing on the pavement waiting for his car to arrive to take him to some event or other, and singing gaily to the doorman the old Tivoli music hall song:

> *I've been to the North Pole,*
> *I've been to the South Pole,*
> *The East Pole, the West Pole,*
> *And every other kind of Pole,*
> *The Barber's Pole,*
> *The greasy Pole,*
> *And now I'm fairly up the Pole,*
> *Since I got the sack*
> *From the Hotel Metropole.*

I do not know that I ever loved him more than in the months that followed. There was no false bravado. He did not try to hide the fact of his painful surprise at his almost total rejection. But you don't go in for politics for gratitude – you do it to get things done, sometimes pleasant things, sometimes unpleasant. Still his mistress had rebuffed and rejected him, publicly and witheringly in the face of the world, but he was still her servant and would withdraw to the perimeter of her affection, ensconce himself firmly at her door and without her even noticing it begin to play once more the role of an ardent suitor and sometimes a cheeky one.

I burst into pent up tears when I heard I was to accompany him to Lake Como for a month's holiday. My mother could not go; though exhausted emotionally, she had to re-create a home for him. Diana was similarly occupied in domestic duties; Randolph and Mary were still on active service abroad. I was available. Though I was still in uniform there was nothing particularly urgent for me to do so I was given a month's leave and set off with him once more, not officially this time, simply as his daughter. Lord Moran, as always, accompanied us.

Field-Marshal Alexander lent us his villa, La Rosa, on Lake Como; it had been his headquarters in the last days of the war and with great thoughtfulness he had found two delightful soldiers, Captains Ozier and Rogers of the 4th Hussars, my father's old regiment, to be his ADCs.

John Ozier was a husky young man who had been through the entire war and had seen much action. I thought him about thirty, but he was only twenty-five. Dunkirk to the Gothic Line via Alamein had physically matured him, but he carried an air of untouched youthfulness when you talked with him. He was intelligent, kind and considerate. Tim Rogers was a leprechaun, slight, sparkling and witty.

My father had been silent and accepting when we arrived at the villa, and I was anxious in case time should lie heavy even in these beautiful surroundings. He had said that he wished to see no one but Alex and Admiral John Cunningham who were to arrive a few days after us. Of course, to be alone with him suited me very well, but I wondered anxiously for how long he would really find Charles, a couple of youthful ADCs and myself sufficient company.

I needn't have worried. Alex had chosen the right young men, they both got on with my father like a house on fire, and I was greatly relieved. But the first night at dinner was something of an ordeal. My father, pink from his bath and immaculately dressed in a white suit, sat at the head of an enormous green glass table in an oval pale green room. There was an impersonal yard or two between us. We were waited upon by four white-coated batmen, and I felt like a goldfish in a bowl.

My father contemplated the two young men with that shattering, silent scrutiny many had come to know. I looked across the table at the two slightly perspiring ADCs in their own agony of nerves in case something should go wrong. Charles was next to me, lost in a coma of philosophical meditation with himself, probably thinking about how many bugs the Italian water he was about to drink contained and whether they would prove fatal or not. I sat next to my father.

The silence was suddenly shattered by my father asking as he glared at the soup, 'Is this soup hot or not?' – 'Hot' we replied in unison. One of the batmen stepped forward, 'Very hot, sir' – 'Humph' grunted my father and picked up his spoon and began to drink it. It was of course tepid. My father gave me the faintest wink, the tension eased. We all knew that the soup would be very hot tomorrow and every following evening; all was going to be well, all in fact was going to be very well.

Night after night Charles and I would sit back comfortably while the boys fought the battles from Omdurman to Alamein.

On September 3rd, 1945, the anniversary of the war's outbreak, I wrote a letter to my mother:

Lake Como

Just six years ago today. . . .

I wish you were here with us. I was so distressed to see you so unhappy and tired when we left and so was he. We never see a lovely sight that he doesn't say 'I wish your mother were here'.

The days are filled with painting and picnics. The first picture was a success, a luminous lake and boats caught in the sunlight at it's foot.

The villa, it is a palace of mirrors. I never know whether I am coming or going as I converge on myself from a hundred different angles. And my bathroom, it is cream and apricot marble. The bath is in the middle of the room like a throne, right in front of long french windows, so that one can see out over the lake to the mountains. It seems all the walls are mirrored, so about six of me step into the apricot bath. It is fun but I don't feel I am alone and the first evening I was convulsed with giggles as a chorus of Sarahs completed their ablutions.

The weather is perfect, by no means too hot as yet. A cool breeze runs round the lake as though to order in the early morning and then again in the late afternoon. The nights are cool and the crickets sing under the windows. We shall be very happy here. Now at last one can sit in the sun without the thought of war sitting beside one.

As for the Italians I search their faces, they are all gay, brown and smiling and seemingly quite untouched by the war. War to them is obviously like everything else in their lives, something physical, a physical catastrophe that happens, is unpleasant, is over and forgotten, like an earthquake, not a moral or an emotional upheaval to be pondered on or a bitter lesson from which something must be learnt. Oh no, the tooth has stopped aching, the sun is shining again. Who won it? Who lost it? Who cares? That was last week, this is today. Look Churchill, Churchill, Viva, viva. Both the young and the old know him. I was astonished at a bunch of children, the eldest not more than twelve, who looked at us calmly and the eldest said 'Churchill'. They can't do enough for us, they bring out chairs to us to sit on, towels to dry our hands with and then retire about twenty yards and sit and watch for hours. Our ADC, I fear, thinks we are too polite. In front of a barrage of smiles it is difficult to be other than cordial, but then suddenly the picture of Mussolini and his mistress in the market square flashes into one's mind. . . .

The days were filled with painting and picnics. I adore picnics, often at formal meals at organized times I feel it impossible to eat, and nibble and push my food round my plate. I eat very little anyway, only one meal a day and sometimes only every other day, but invite me to a picnic and I give you fair warning now that I'll eat you out of every paper bag in sight, and then may be found scrabbling about the bottom of the basket in case anything has been overlooked.

Picnics played a great part in our holiday life throughout the years; in fact whenever I think back to holidays with my parents, no matter what part of the globe we might go to, picnics formed,it seems in remembrance, the main adventure of the holiday. Before one of them I would let my mind dwell happily on the food. These picnics were planned as carefully as a banquet or a military operation. Eggs in aspic always a must, you got your little pot with a spoon and you could wander round and talk to people or admire the scenery, then you took it back and got cold roast beef galantine or chicken, mostly eaten with fingers: cucumber salad, celery and radishes; Stilton cheese and biscuits; cool white wine, coffee in a thermos. Brandy for the men and then, across the delicate perfumed air of whatever part of the world we were in, would float the inevitable smell of cigar.

So there were picnics now, and my father was relaxed. Adamant as he had to be, as any man must be at times, he had the disarming quality of looking over his mistakes with an acceptance, balancing his debt overwhelmingly in favour of the departed opponent.

Without anyone really knowing, he would go about repairing any hurt feelings, except where there was no honour and people deliberately lied or cheated or bore false witness, then there was no recourse.

When he was eighty years old, the nation gave him a party and pocket-money 'sans tax' to spend. He had all the fun of a schoolboy planning what he would do with the money. So much for this . . . so much for that . . . so much for . . . No. How could he take it – but give it back?

In my mother he found an undiminishing star. 'Mule,' he would nudge me at a gathering (using his private nickname for me), 'at her best no one can beat her.' We would hold hands on that in silent pact. And now back to the accounts. '£x for butterflies,' he said suddenly. 'I hope the National Trust have remembered to bring in the special plants at Chartwell that butterflies like to live on. . . .'

Painting was often to save my father's temper and mind.

September 8th, 1945   Lake Como
Darling Mummie,

Time flies too quickly, we have already been here a week. He is looking tremendously well and is much happier with every lovely picture and they are really lovely. Care slips away, we've had no newspapers or letters for five days, he was completely resigned about the newspapers, not so about the letters. Thank goodness Alex arrived and brought a lovely one from you. Alex can only stay one day which is very sad but long enough to do one lovely picture. They painted the same scene. It is amazing how their styles are very similar and the painting conversation has been a delight. It roughly goes like this, Alex: 'I always use just a touch of Rose Madder, do you use Rose Madder, Winston?' – 'But of course, I always use Rose Madder, what about Yellow Ochre?' Alex: 'Yes, yes I'm very fond of Yellow Ochre, Yellow Ochre pale is very useful. I tell you what I really like, one shouldn't use it but I always like a touch of pure black on the palette.' Winston: 'Ah now there I disagree with you, no black, Neutral Tint perhaps, but never black. Do you know Neutral Tint? You don't? My dear Alex you must try Neutral Tint, much better than black. I don't like the sepulchral finality of black. I must say I like bright colours. [As he wrote later 'I rejoice with the brilliant ones, and am genuinely sorry for the poor browns. When I get to heaven I mean to spend a considerable portion of my first million years in painting, and so get to the bottom of the subject. But then I shall require a still gayer palette than I get here below. I expect orange and vermilion will be the darkest, dullest colours upon it and beyond them there will be a whole range of wonderful new colours which will delight the celestial eye.'[1]] And so on and so on. Last night I heard them wandering around the house theoretically touching up the positively frightful pictures there and Papa saying, 'Now come here, Alex, come here, now really look at this, we really paint better than the bastard who painted this one.' I really think he is over it, it is hard to tell, but he said last night: 'Every day I stay here without news, without worry I realize more and more that it may very well be what your mother said, a blessing in disguise. The war is over, it is won and they have lifted the hideous aftermath from my shoulders. I am what I never thought I would be until I reached my grave "sans soucis et sans regrets".' The only thing he misses is you.

Yesterday before we started out with Alex for a painting picnic we were told that there were two little

[1] From the essay 'Painting as a Pastime', by Winston Churchill (Odhams Press).

girls clutching bouquets of wilting flowers in their hands, waiting to give them to Papa and that they had been there for hours and hours, and spirits and flowers and white muslin dresses were all drooping. Papa naturally asked them in and they shyly presented their posies, enormous bunches of gladioli as big as themselves; a touching little scene, but no sooner over than the real reason emerged, a blonde and attractive Italian woman leapt into the scene and started to gush. The children having accomplished their mission were swept away and the blonde, we supposed proud mama, started off on a great eulogy about Papa. Papa politely listened for a few gushes and then with incredible ability lured Alex from the balcony and said: 'Madame, I feel you should shower some of your kindness on your real liberator, the Supreme Commander of the Allied Forces.' The blonde lady without a pause, without a blush, started again: 'I am so full of respect and admiration, yes the children are sweet. No, quiet Lucy, no they are not mine, they are my friend's there, over there in the corner' (a dim smirking unattractive brunette was suddenly revealed in the corner). 'She too is full of respect and admiration but does not speak English good. Always I listen to the English broadcast, always I thought the Allies would win.' 'Yes I thought so too,' said Field-Marshal Alexander, bowing slightly and with the nicest of smiles and in his gentlest manner. . . .

There were, indeed, some perfectly frightful pictures in the house, and one above all he sat and stared at every evening. It was of a stagnant murky pool and reflected some

Lake Como,
by Sir Winston Churchill

funereal shrubbery. Two sombre fir trees blotted out much of the sky which looked reminiscent of a London fog, and peering biliously between the trees was a pale and sickly sun. That picture became the butt and focus of Alex and my father the evening they were together. After Alex had left, Papa was sitting staring as usual at the offending picture, when suddenly turning to us he said: 'We are all agreed, are we not, that this is the worst picture that has ever been painted?' We murmured assent. 'It takes the palm, the prize for bad pictures; you must say it's offensive?' Again we nodded our assent. In a twinkling of an eye the picture was off the wall, was prised out of its frame and was being carried triumphantly up to the bathroom, which was being used as a studio, to be doctored. Charles groaned: 'He oughtn't to do it, he oughtn't to do it.' 'Oughtn't he?' I asked. 'No,' said Charles, 'but you won't stop him,' and taking up the banner of passive resistance, went off to bed.

I leapt upstairs where my father was squeezing great daubs of vivid colour. The two boys sat on the edge of the bath goggle-eyed. I delivered my lecture: 'You really mustn't,' I said. As the first vivid red hit the gloomy canvas my voice trailed away, suddenly beautiful flaming azaleas appeared on the dingy shrubbery, the dingy firs were given back the new green of their youth, the pallid sun instead of trying to break through the fog with fitful gleam sank in a splurge of glory, and the fog as if by magic disappeared, and the happiest of blue skies smiled down on the whole scene which had been caught by the hitherto stagnant, repellent pool, now a kaleidoscope of reflections. It was breathtaking, it was enchanting, it was lovely. The whole thing accomplished and back in its frame and back on the wall inside half an hour, we sat and admired it for two hours, exhausted but satisfied by this act of 'artistic rape' as my father called it.

Early next morning, one by one we tiptoed down to have a look. What would the morning light reveal? Well do you know, it was still lovely, it glowed brazenly like a bird of paradise and we were all heart-broken when it was once more carried upstairs to have its face washed. It now hangs back on the wall, stagnant and gloomy as before.

This holiday was, for me, one of the happiest. Perhaps it was the relief, I don't know, but we had the time of our lives and he seemed happy.

One night we were sitting after dinner looking out across the lake. The silence broken only by the goat bells, the stars dimmed in the velvet of the night by the peaceful flaring of his cigar. Suddenly he said: 'Out of a life of long and varied experience, the most valuable piece of advice I could hand on to you is to know how to command the moment to remain.' – 'That is what I am trying to do now, sir,' said John Ozier with complete sincerity and simplicity.

Now we were nearing St Paul's Cathedral. I remembered seeing it silhouetted in flames from the roof of the Savoy, standing by my father's side . . . all those years ago. . . .

We had been told it was not necessary to curtsey to the Queen and her family. They were already in their pews. For the first time in English history, the monarch waived her prerogative and waited for her humble servant.

He loved Chartwell – at one time both he and my mother had planned to be buried there, near his poodles, Rufus I and Rufus II. But one day, a few years before, the idea came to him to return to his birthplace – he had survived almost a century, and his thoughts as he wandered round Blenheim that day must have been all-embracing, for he decided to commit his bones to the earth where his beloved father and mother and brother Jack awaited him. . . .

The Battle Hymn of the Republic crashed through the great cathedral, as the bombs had crashed around it in 1940. . . . Ghosts? they only live in our desire . . . it is perhaps our memories that see the mist hover over the lake and fireflies dance where no human could. . . . He is gone . . . a barge did come and carry him on . . . the steel cranes bowed their heads . . . the gull-grey sky held and the Thames ran softly on. . . . He is gone. What is mortal of him lies at Bladon. . .

Forgive Me

Forgive me if I do not cry
The day you die,
Streams at some seasons
Wind their way through country lanes of beauty
And are dry.

The willow bends its head
To kiss the empty river bed
With the same caress it gave
When in its heyday it was full and high
Oh river know that I remember
The splashing laughing clatter
Of a bubbling day in Spring
When everything was blossoming!

Butterflies still hover
Down the rocky bed
And weeds grow strong and
Guard the pebbled way.
In this high noon of nothing
Which is death
Brave flags still wave
Cowslip-parsley, rag weed and sorrel
Shout to me
That Spring is on her way
Comfort, I am still too deaf to hear.

Yet forgive me if I do not cry
The day you die
The simplest reason that I know
You said you'd rather have it so
And that I held my head serenely high
Remembering the love and glory that we knew.
Forgive me if I do not cry
The day you die. . . .
Forgive me
If I do. . . .